How to Implement Computers in a Small to Medium-Size Business

Clive Libotte. IEng. MInstMC

How to Implement Computers in a Small to Medium-Size Business

Published by TRAMCAR - *bringing you professional knowledge.*

Contact TRAMCAR at clibotte@optusnet.com.au. Perth, Western Australia. Document Number P90.01.19. Version 3.3. 15 December 2011.

Produced with Free Open Source Software (FOSS). Typeset with LyX 1.6.7. The Document Processor, http://www.lyx.org. Book cover design set out with Scribus Desktop Publishing, http://www.scribus.net. Drawings produced with Open Office Draw, http://openoffice.org. Free cover graphic image from http://www.vector-portal.com.

Where to obtain this book. The international book distributers Amazon.com BarnsandNoble.com and Ingram Book Company make this book available worldwide in hard and electronic copy on the Internet.

ISBN 978-0-646-55559-1

Disclaimer. This book describes a management process widely accepted in engineering disciplines as representing current best management practice. It requires the application of management skills and judgement for its successful completion. Therefore the author and publisher assume no responsibility for the outcome obtained with respect to any loss or damage as a result of applying the methods described herein. In addition, while every care has been taken to make this book as complete and accurate as practicable, the author and publisher assume no liability for errors or omissions that may exist in the book.

After conceiving an idea, implementation takes up to eighty per
cent of the task to bring it to
fruition - plan for the best, allow
for the worst, and deal with the
unexpected.

Who should read this book

- Small and medium-size business owners or staff who have the responsibility of purchasing a new or replacement business computer system and who are not information technology professionals.

About this book

- This book describes the process of defining a computer system in terms of business objectives and transforming them into a requirement specification and purchasing contract.

- It is a management guide, which is largely independent of the technology adopted, therefore it will not become obsolescent.

- The language is mostly non-technical, so the book can be used by non-technical people.

- It gives sound advice beyond that given by many business support organisations; it gives business owners, management and staff the knowledge and skill that will serve them for the remainder of their careers.

Read this book to learn how to:

- Manage the implementation process by providing an explanation of major steps, complete with examples of the key documents that you will need to complete your project successfully.

- Specify a computer system based on the accumulated experience of information managers and engineering professionals.

- Gain the advantages of purchasing a commercial-off-the-shelf computer system, with its lower development risk, reduced hardware and software costs and straightforward day-to-day maintenance.

- Provide timely and relevant business information to distant customers and local staff, reducing business operating costs.

- Choose a suitable vendor and manage vendor relationships to avoid misunderstandings and prevent procurement delays.

Contents

List of Figures

List of Tables

Introduction

Since business adopted computers during the nineteen-seventies, the consensus is that computer systems have had a beneficial effect on the efficacy of business organisations. The development of the personal computer caused a migration of computing machines from the scientific and military worlds into the business and domestic worlds of ordinary people. Since that migration, the reliance on computer systems for successful business operation and the delivery of services continues to increase, showing no sign of abatement. As managing a business becomes more demanding because of regulatory pressures relating to privacy, safety, quality, discrimination, unfair-trade, finance, taxation, increased local and international competition, and the rising expectations of customers for personal attention, then the need for effective information management to withstand these pressures has demanded the adoption of computer systems into many areas of business activity. This generates the need to clearly specify the information needs of the business and hence the requirements of the computer system, so that it supports the expected business objectives. Spending time creating the documentation, consisting of a contract and a requirements specification, is an essential element in the technology procurement process.

Useful business information requires the collection of data from a number of different business activities, so its computers need to be connected together to share the data. The standard way of connecting local computers together is though a Local Area Network (LAN). More widespread connections are also needed to connect to distant computers on the Wide Area Networks (WANs) of the business world. These networks are needed to access customers, suppliers, and professional institutions and also for collaboration with sub-contractors and consultants. The network provides the facility for sharing information. It is this access to otherwise isolated sources of information that enables the business to become more effective in the delivery of customer care; and to manage a wide range of complex administrative tasks brought about by the necessity of operating in the demanding commercial environment of today's business. The ease in which information is found, delivered to and assimilated by the user is a measure of the success of a networked computer system. This success is heavily dependent upon the way the system is specified and brought into being, as it has a marked effect on the project outcome.

The advantages of purchasing a commercial-off-the-shelf, as opposed to a custom designed system are: lower capital investment, because its components are standard low-cost mass produced parts; lower development risk, because its hardware and software are thoroughly developed and tested for a known mass market; and simple operational maintenance, because of the ready availability of trained service technicians. Some examples of business activities which have been successfully computerised with commercial-off-the-shelf computers are accounting, administration, design engineering, graphic arts, management, marketing, sales, quality assurance, and recruitment. Computerisation has also been successful in non-profit-making activities such as those found in charities, aid organisations and schools. Although these non-profit organisations are not strictly business entities, the way in which they are managed are becoming more and more business-like to enable them to survive in the current regulatory environment. Computers have also moved into areas such as manufacturing, product supply chains and process plant, but activities in these industries are typically undertaken by trained professionals.

Engineers of all disciplines learn the art and science of specifying, bringing into being, and testing technological products and systems. Oil rigs, aircraft, cars, lawn mowers, washing machines and other modern devices, all share a common and well understood management process in their creation — the management of the design process. General computer systems, which manage business information, also require the application of that common management process to obtain the many benefits available from them.

The main concern of business in the management of the design process is to clearly express its objectives though the requirements specification — the vendor will do the rest. The following chapters will show you how to specify what you require, interact with vendors, evaluate their quotations, and get the system installed and tested to your satisfaction.

Management Issues and How to Get Started

People, Work and Information

Look at the problem this way. A computer system is a tool for information management and computation. Principally you are in the position of wanting to solve business problems, making your business more productive and efficient at meeting customer needs. A computer system is one of the tools, amongst others, that you can use for this purpose. Follow the advice below to ensure that the computer system that you procure supports your business objectives rather than undermines them. Think firstly about your customers, secondly about the people in your organisation, thirdly about the nature of the business, and fourthly about the information needs of everyone. After completing this activity — you can productively think about the technicalities of the system, but these are best left to the vendor's system designers.

Change Management

Implementing (or upgrading) a computer system involves change in the way people work and think, therefore it's an exercise in change management. Most people are likely to experience some level of anxiety about the unknown. They want to know how the changes will affect their working day; will they have more or less responsibility, will their standing in the business be changed, will they even remain with the organisation? In addition, the people staffing a business already know a great deal about the productivity problems that a business harbours. They experience them every working day — poor communication between people or departments; delays in obtaining or complete lack of vital business information; convoluted methods of data entry; crashing or freezing software; slow or non-existent technical support; uncomfortable physical conditions; noise; lack of time to complete a task properly (leaving unfortunate colleagues to tie up the loose ends later) and many, many more. This business knowledge is a valuable resource and you need to collect it to improve business productivity. You can allay people's fear of change, secure their co-operation and collect valuable productivity ideas by involving them directly in the process of identifying the business needs. Often called (obviously) *Needs Analysis,* but this process also goes under names such as Business Analysis or Systems Analysis. Note that this process forms the foundation of a useful requirements specification and is largely separate from the later technical activities.

Whether it's a new installation or an upgrade, bring your people together and explain the overall objectives of computerisation to them (in effect, a provisional project plan — see project management later). Because this process of involvement is an iterative one, and people need time to develop and clarify their ideas, you will need a series of meetings, where initially the objective will be to collect ideas and opinions of involved staff. Combine this collective staff wisdom with the objectives of your business so that you can see its information management needs, formalise these into a computer system requirements specification. Pay particular attention to the software needs of the end-users, and later on in the process encourage them to trial proposed software and act on their observations. There is more detail on how to conduct productive meetings later on in this chapter, and the chapter *'Obtaining Your Specified Needs'* has an example of a requirement specification.

Needs Analysis

The essential first step is to think, in a business sense, about what you *really, really need!* Do this by stating the benefits you expect from the computer network expressed in terms of business objectives. Avoid the common tendency to shop from a list of technological products without a clear idea of the business outcomes that you plan to achieve. Start with the vision statement of your business. If you have no vision statement then use this project as a stimulus to write one. Here is a sample (and simple) vision statement. 'We *[name of business]* commit to providing timely, ethical, state-of-the-art and friendly customer service. In pursuit of this commitment we shall generate a professional and supportive work environment for management, staff and trainees. We shall maintain the business as a profitable long-term enterprise to secure the continuation of our customer services.' Vision statements appear in many different forms, and because of their nature, have a content that is general in scope. Nevertheless, they encapsulate the culture of the business and should represent its true objectives; don't allow your marketing people too much freedom of input, as customers will soon detect any serious discrepancy between the reality of dealing with your business and any hyperbolic statements contained in your vision statement. When you have a vision statement, divide the business into operational areas and describe the objectives of each area to support the vision statement.

It's helpful to think in terms of information management. Is there a large amount of detailed information you need to store to do a particular task? This becomes a database. Are there other databases outside the business to which you require access? This requires connection to external networks. How many people need access to the databases? How many will be denied access? Do you want staff to communicate with one another electronically inside the business? This becomes internal email. By asking a series of work-related questions you can build a picture of your needs, which is the basis of the requirements specification.

Keep asking until you have collected everyone's needs — manage this analysis with vigour until you have exhausted everyone's ideas, so that in the future, no one in the organisation can claim that they were not consulted! Although the initial analysis will be flexible and iterative in nature, get the team participants to express their needs in writing as the ideas become firm. Human beings have a perverse habit of changing their minds over time and claiming their new needs are the same as those expressed in the past. Use the example *'Requirements Specification'* in the chapter *'Obtaining Your Specified Needs'* as a basis for ideas. Separately, here is an incomplete list of some common operational areas for computerisation:

- Accounting and Finance. General purpose accounting and business cash flow, financial modeling.

- Office Administration. Word processing, electronic document control and internal and external communications.

- Customer Service. Marketing, sales, order entry and order tracking to delivery.

- Supply Chain. Purchasing materials, tracking delivery into warehouse and stock control.

- Design. Computer aided design in all engineering disciplines and graphical arts.

- Manufacturing. Production control, job allocation and order fulfillment from sales input.

- Professional Services. Customer resource allocation and charging.

The available business resources will dictate how much of the business can be changed from manual operation to computerised operation at one time, or, if the business is already computerised, how much of the system can be upgraded at one time. If you decide to computerise a part of your business, keep in mind that each element of the system must be able to be connected to future elements: the system should be *scalable* (able to be expanded). Your network will tend towards expansion as your computing experience and your business grow.

Quantify the improvements that you expect to gain from the computer network in one or more of the operational areas. Some of these improvements may not be measurable in a mathematical sense, but they may enable you to do something that was not possible before, or they may make existing tasks more convenient. It is important to make the improvements measurable or at least observable, so that you can assess the efficacy of the system later.

There is a tendency to avoid the needs analysis stage of the project simply because it involves a lot of detailed thinking, but when completed it does make the remainder of the project easier to manage and the outcome more certain; so you will be glad of it later.

One of the initial steps in deciding the project scope is to choose the *type* of software application that you intend to use (the system vendor will propose software brands in their response to your 'request for a quotation'). The task of deciding which type of software you need requires a contradictory approach. You have to know the capability of current software applications before you can realistically say what type of software you will require. You will most likely need additional specialist information such as: subscription newsletters which are concerned only with business software reviews; Internet sites which cater for business software in your industry; books dedicated to the subject; your nearby business colleagues; and finally, consultants who specialize in selecting business software. A useful tip for software to reduce the amount of initial comparison is to see if the software is in your country's "Top Ten" in one of the above resources. This can save you a lot of time. The other initial step in deciding the scope of the project are: choose the people in your business who will have a workstation (a personal computer and associated peripherals), and how many types of software applications they will be using. I will tell you more about this in the chapter *'Obtaining Your Specified Needs'*.

Work-flow

The way people work together changes when you migrate from manual to electronic communication. Users take a different approach to access information, employing different methods to communicate with one another, the information flows by different routes. So setting up a networked computer system to secure productivity gains involves changing the way people interact with one another, as well as establishing their interaction with the computer system. This task forms a considerable part of the work of the project team in addition to any of the technical issues they have to deal with. Solve the business issues first, get a grasp of the software capabilities available on the computer network, then devise new ways of working together productively.

One effective way of describing work-flow processes is to use an illustration in the form of a work-flow diagram. You can simply use a large sheet paper, and draw the information flow and the associated events, actions and tasks. There are software applications designed specifically to do this job, but computer screens are rarely large enough for the whole process to be appreciated. When you have finished with the discussions, and the hand drawing, then, if you feel the need for neatness, turn the work over to a software application designed for the task.

You will need to examine the work-flow of each major business process. Look at how you do things now, and compare it to the business objectives you have identified during the Needs Analysis exercise. Set limits to the extent, and the amount of detail of each business process analysis: otherwise it snakes throughout your business and seems endless. You can devise the work-flow diagram in layers with the top layer showing the major processes only, and then if necessary, produce a more detailed work-flow chart of each major process below (figuratively speaking). Do one at time, listening to the people directly involved, changing the work-flow acting on their feedback. This will enhance the overall effectiveness of the process. Not every person will get exactly what they want, but the objective should be to simplify the process, enhance quality, raise productivity, reduce costs and improve customer service. Fig 1 shows an example of a work-flow diagram. When you have the computer system installed and working, trial each work-flow design and review the results. When you have resolved any problems, formalise the new process by writing work procedures and flow diagrams for future reference.

Information Management

Guidance. [*Information management is a neglected subject. Many people think that somehow the computer software will take care of everything. Well, the software will have a strong influence on way information flows though the organisation, but it will not take care of the document characteristics which enhance the communication between human beings such as: identification, appropriate content, graphical presentation, uniformity, currency, and availability. You have to define these characteristics yourself if you want your computer system to be productive. Also, don't think that information management is a discipline only for large companies, a single person business needs information management policies based on the list below. If you do not organise your business information, then your computer system will automate business chaos at high speed.*]

The *existence* of your business relies upon the information contained within it. The *success* of your business depends upon the useful manipulation and delivery of information to your business staff and the customers and regulators outside the business. Whatever the size of your business you need an information management policy, without which your computer system will never realize its full potential. This policy will describe the method of handling information in the organisation and will cover the following aspects of information management:

- Delivery. Define the information each user needs to view; determine if they need to edit, annotate and search the information supplied. As well as the internal business users, here you will have to include users from outside parties, such as financial, safety and privacy regulators.

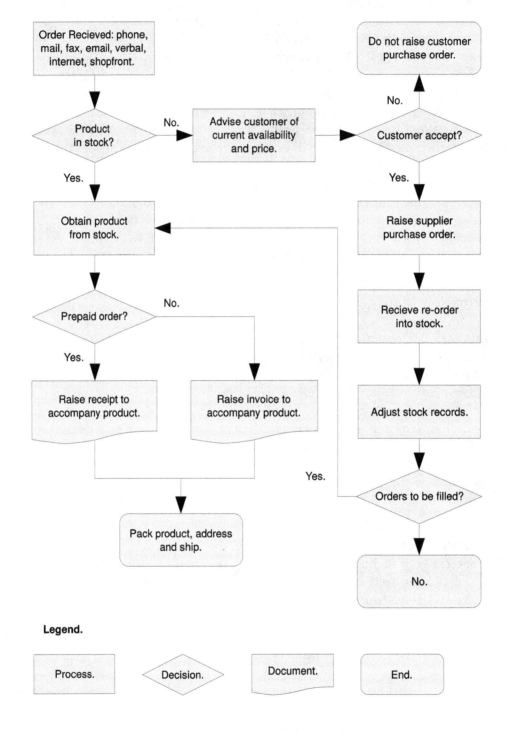

Figure 1: A Work-flow Diagram

- Capture. Specify how the information will be captured from internal creation and outside sources. The capture point is *the* place to apply control of the information for authorisation, search-indexing and version control.

- Storage, Security and Backup. Decide where the information will reside. Will it be in one place such as on a network server, or in a number of places such as on user workstations or the Internet? Most likely you will need the main part of the information on a server (or servers) and other parts on workstations or the Internet. Storage includes security, backup and disaster recovery plans.

- Identification. Uniquely identify the documents which hold the information whether on paper or electronic media, otherwise you cannot manage them without confusion. Specify the categories of documents and the relationship between them (if any) and *standardize* the naming and numbering system for the processing of all documents throughout your business.

- Distribution. Decide how the information will be shared between individuals and groups of people. Groups of people with specialised shared interests such as administration, engineering, finance, marketing and production for instance, will need unrestricted access to their own data which is of little interest to others. Alternatively some business-wide processes (work-flow) such as order fulfillment will require tracking by a number of groups or individuals, and therefore require equal access by everyone involved in the process. Think about how information will be released from the system, internally and externally through electronic means and printing. Who will authorise internal and external documents for release?

- Retention and Disposal. Who will decide how long to keep the documents and when to dispose of them. National legislation controls the management of many types of business documents, and will determine the content of some of your information management policies.

- Training. To implement the policies you have created you will need to write procedures for training users how the policies work in business. Keep the documents up-to-date in line with changing policies, so that users can be retrained to maintain company policy in the future.

To obtain more practical detail of this subject for your industry sector, approach your business association, a government business help organisation, your learned profession institution or a consultant with expertise in this subject in your industry.

In practice, the activities of dealing with change management, needs analysis, work-flow and information management are combined into one integrated activity as each one is closely bound to the others into a single business process.

Project Management

One prevalent cause of project failure in the adoption of technological products is poor management, rather than poor engineering. For the business procuring a computer system, there are two management elements in which you are directly involved. One is the determination of your needs resulting in a concise requirements specification, and the other is the overall management of the implementation process by means of the contract (which includes the requirements specification). If the requirements specification is not clear to the vendor, then no amount of engineering ingenuity by the vendor will meet the end-user's expectations. If the vendor isn't guided by the contract during the design and implementation process, then the probability that the vendor will deviate from the end-user's wishes increases as the project unfolds. The way in which you, the end-user, gets directly involved in the two management elements, so that the result is what you expect, is described below. The chapter *'Obtaining Your Specified Needs'* shows examples of the documents involved.

Devise a Written Project Plan

A project plan promotes logical thought and discussion; enables you to resolve problems early while they are still manageable; and helps people deal with the emotional adjustments caused by workplace changes. Its great strength is that it promotes resource allocation — do people have the skills and time to complete their tasks by the scheduled dates? A project plan can be as simple as a list of people assigned to recognisable tasks against calendar dates, or you can use sophisticated project control software designed for the purpose. It depends upon the complexity of the project and the computer skills of participating group members. There is an example of a typical project plan in the chapter *'Obtaining Your Specified Needs'*.

Form a Project Group and Allocate Responsibilities

Gather the business members together. Explain the objectives of the project in broad terms, and choose the members of the project team. Each person in the newly formed project team will want to know what part they are to play as the project unfolds. Make this clear by assigning each person a range of responsibilities, both technical and managerial, which they have to shoulder during the *implementation* process. Point out that these responsibilities are temporary and different to those which will be required during the permanent *operation* of the network.

Apart from the technical tasks there are three key project positions: the project manager, the meeting chairperson and the meeting minutes-taker. If your business is large enough, allocate these duties to separate persons. Their duties are as follows:

- The project leader draws up the project plan showing the major activities, events and time-scales; allocates tasks and responsibilities to project team members; resolves political differences; monitors progress and helps remove administrative obstacles; co-ordinates the various tasks so that they complement one another, so avoiding duplication of effort; ensures that project information flows between project members and external organisations.

- The project meeting chairperson arranges regular project meetings, gathering the participants together to make the meeting a reality; once at the meeting, keeps everyone's minds and conversations focused on project task completion (task follow-up); encourages new ideas for the solution of organisational problems; transfers detailed technical subjects to be solved outside the meeting by a smaller or different group of people; deals with the different personality types at the meeting so that each person has an equal opportunity to make a contribution; and brings the meeting to a close.

- The minutes-taker draws up the meeting agenda and distributes them to the participants several days before the meeting takes place; takes the minutes at the meetings; writes the minutes up and distributes then to the participants soon after the close of the meeting.

Although the duties are described in isolation, in practice they will need to be done in a spirit of co-operation between members of the project team. The principal skills required of the project leader are managerial, of the chairperson, people-handling and of the minutes-taker, administrative.

Meetings

Running effective meetings is an essential part of project management and the only way that project information can flow to all participants is though the distributed copies of the minutes. Remember that there may be interested parties outside the business boundaries, such as vendors, consultants and information technology officers. Ensure that they get copies as appropriate. There are formal and informal meetings. The formal meetings will, in general, consist of the full project team; the informal, of two or three people dealing with technical matters that require resolution away from the formal meetings. The guidance given below applies to formal meetings, but bear the guidelines in mind when you are having informal meetings — if you want to socialize do it during your coffee-break or lunch-break. Here are the guidelines for successful meetings.

- Plan on holding project meetings once a fortnight: this is the optimum frequency to allow sufficient time for actions to be resolved — and insufficient time for participants to forget they are members of the project team.

- State the objectives of the meeting beforehand in measurable or observable outcomes. Project meetings are chiefly progress meetings to exchange information, and initiate and conclude project tasks.

- Take minutes of *agreed actions — not detail.* The minutes should include a brief description of the required action, the person responsible for resolving it (following-up), the action, and the time scale involved for completion.

- Distribute the minutes immediately after the meeting. This gives participants time to think, act and make a contribution at the next meeting.

The minutes-taker has an onerous task, because listening and writing at the same time is not an easy activity to complete successfully. You are fortunate if you have any volunteers for this job. Meeting members should support the minutes-taker by pausing in their deliberations to assist in the recording of the agreed actions (rather than the conversations) of the meeting. Write the minutes up and distribute them immediately after the meeting is closed; otherwise the day-to-day duties of the business cause them to be delayed until just before the next meeting. This gives meeting members insufficient time to follow up their actions, and gather their thoughts together to make a useful contribution at the next meeting: as a result it becomes largely a waste of time.

If the people with the qualities for the key project positions do not have computer knowledge, train them so that they can handle the technical aspects of the job. You cannot, in business, easily change a person's personality: but it is straightforward in comparison to arrange for them to acquire technical knowledge; after which time they will be able to do the job well. Computerisation case histories show that there are considerable additional time-demands on business participants while computer systems are being implemented. The extra workload of project members during this time can be partially offset by hiring part-time staff assistants.

Finance

Financial justification is always a problem with information technology projects. Since you may not have an accurate costing of the system in the initial stages of planning, make estimates by studying similar business case histories; talk to members of your local business association, professional learned society or government business assistance unit. Often these organisations have specialized information technology groups within them; they are ready to help. Be sure to include estimates of the cost of training for all the involved members of your business as well as the system hardware, software and maintenance.

There are regular periods when governments formulate new polices to improve the national small and medium-size business performance. If you meet certain conditions, none of which are onerous; they provide free expertise as an encouragement to computerise. This expertise relieves you of a substantial part of the system cost and will help you formulate a financial justification. Apart from using your own money, consider the alternative methods of finance such as hire purchase and lease.

Your financial adviser will talk to you about the return-on-investment of the initial cost of a computer system. The basis of such a calculation is that the computer system saves productive time and improves customer service. This increases the overall efficiency of the business bringing down operating costs. The measurable outcome of this would be that the business would service more customers with the same staff resources. Whether or not you have the figures available in your business to do the calculations depends upon its organisational culture — did you collect past data? So what is to be done to make a business case out of computerisation? Go to the business organisations mentioned in the first paragraph of this section, and seek out formal studies on computerisation return-on-investment in the small to medium-size business. Use the results of these studies to satisfy yourself and your financial adviser that computerisation is worth while in a financial context.

People's Time

Do you and your team have time to complete this project? The conceptualisation stage of any project takes between ten and twenty percent of total project time; leaving the remainder, between eighty and ninety per cent for implementation. Although in business these two project phases will occur contemporaneously, most of the conceptualisation takes place in the early stages of the project. Conceptualisation largely consists of the thinking processes: design and planning. Implementation largely of the doing processes: discussion meetings, writing specifications, reports and new procedures, figuring out new work processes, allocating new responsibilities and reallocating existing ones.

The most common cause of failure of attempts at organisational change — for computerisation is organisational change — is individual's lack of time to complete their tasks in a satisfactory manner. Be realistic about the time people have available to attend to their project duties, considering it is in addition to their normal work-load. Seek help if you are time-poor. The computing groups of many business, professional and government organisations have information technology officers who are available part-time to assist with many aspects of computerisation. Alternatively hire an independent outside consultant to carry out specific parts of the programme. But, initially, do not rely heavily on the hardware or software vendors as their agenda is different from yours, and their interpretation of your needs may not coincide with your expectations.

Training

Once you have allocated responsibilities, decide who needs training. Start early: at least six months ahead of the time you require your network to be on-line, more if you can. The reason for this is that even if your project participants are already computer-literate, they will still need additional knowledge about new software and network issues. And this knowledge will be invaluable to them during implementation when they are reviewing new software and writing the requirements specification. The smaller the business the greater the training problem. If no-one can be spared from normal duties to attend formal training courses, then consider alternatives such as: CDs or DVDs training material, Internet training, and remember, it is still hard to beat a good book on the subject. These alternatives have the advantage that participants can train in a way that suits their work commitments; but be prepared for the longer training periods required, compared to instructor-led classroom training.

Selecting a System Vendor (Supplier)

When you are looking for a vendor for the first time, it does seem a daunting task because there are many unknowns and uncertainties. Get help to do this. The first step is to reduce the size of the problem to a manageable proportion. Try the following resources: your business association, a government business help organisation, and your learned professional institution. Another way is to reduce the number of vendors who *qualify* to be considered for the privilege of supplying you with hardware and software. Narrow down the field using the following questions on the vendors that look promising to you (the qualification process). The answers to most of the questions below should be 'yes' for qualification.

Before you start it is useful to have some idea on how the industry is organised. At the top level of expertise there are a relatively small number of organisations who participate in supplying both large and small businesses with hardware, software and services; they do research and development and work closely with government, academia and not-for-profit organisations to support communities internationally. These top level companies have *partners,* also known as *value-added resellers* (VARs). The partners are arranged into a world-wide network of vendors able to provide technical and commercial services to local customers. The top level organisations ensure that their partners have a high standard of technical and commercial expertise, so that they are able to serve customers as if the customers were dealing with the high level organisation. It's a form of commercial quality accreditation. There are also many independent, competent vendors world-wide — it depends where you are located. A number of these independent vendors who are not directly associated with a major vendor will have *independent* quality system accreditation obtained from a national quality accreditation body:

- Does the vendor (or partner) design, develop and support the products in your country? Or, if not, has the vendor established a partner network in your country committed to supporting its products?

- Is the vendor geographically close enough to provide realistic support?

- How long has the vendor conducted business. Does the vendor have sufficient financial strength to stay in business?

- Have business regulators, associations, standards, quality and government authorities had input into the vendor's quality management system? Does the vendor have quality system accreditation?

- Has the vendor's products been used successfully in businesses similar to yours elsewhere?

- Could you form a trustworthy, open and long-term relationship with the vendor?

Some of the above criteria are subjective, but you should be able to produce a short list of say three vendors after applying it. When you have chosen three vendors, the next essential steps go like this:

- Write your contract and system requirements specification.

- Send these documents requesting a quotation to the three chosen system vendors.

- Compare the returned quotations and make your choice.

- Engage the selected vendor to complete the work according to the project plan. When you reach this stage it is time to refine you assessment. To do this you will need to visit the vendor and discuss your needs in more detail.

If possible, during the selection process choose a vendor who has all the skills needed to complete the project. This is the ideal situation. If the selected vendor needs sub-contractors to complete the project, then be sure to specify in your contact that you will deal only with the selected vendor. State that the selected vendor, now called the principal vendor, is completely responsible for the performance of the sub-contractors. Examples of sub-contractors are software and hardware suppliers and training providers.

Dealing with the System Vendor

The contract and the requirements specification form the basis of good communication between the business and the vendor. It contains the business objectives, computer network features, functions, quantities and limitations from the *end-user* point of view. It does not contain the technical details on *how* the features, functions, quantities and limitations will be achieved; that is a network design task for the vendors to deal with in their formal quotations. In addition it describes the utilities such as telecommunications services and power supplies that are required to support network operation. It ensures that all the vendors understand your needs and so quote against common information. This makes it possible to make a meaningful comparison between vendors. It also enables you to control changes in the network specification; and it gives you a document for acceptance testing before formal hand-over. Once the network is handed over to the client the vendor expects full payment (but subject to initial support and maintenance agreements).

If It's All Too Much

Writing a contract and a system requirements specification is not a trivial task. The consultation with your people, the technical research, the software and hardware reviewing, and the consulting with potential vendors, all takes time and energy. If you are a small business that does not have the capacity to produce a written contract for yourselves, then most system vendors will supply a standard contract and a pro-forma requirements questionnaire (usually tailored to industry sectors). Here you fill in the blanks by simply ticking boxes. This can serve as a basis for negotiation. It relieves you of the task of producing a formal written document. But you must first carry out the needs analysis and think about information management policies just as if you were producing a written contract; otherwise you will have little idea of which boxes to tick. Do not take the availability of a standard contract as a signal to accept the vendor's terms without challenge. You will still need a number of meetings with the vendor to resolve contractual matters to the satisfaction of both parties.

Relating to the Vendor

The success of your computer network in helping you run your business will not only depend on the competence and capacity of the chosen vendor, but also on the quality of the relationship that develops between you. At the onset, foster a positive, open and productive relationship between yourselves by assigning clear responsibilities to each party. It should be understood that you are relying upon the vendor's technical expertise for the supply and operation of the network. This will ensure that both parties are clear about the part they have to play in the business relationship. You will deal with the vendor though informal and formal means. There will be face-to-face conversations, telephone calls, letters, emails, contracts and specifications: conduct all these exchanges with courtesy and professionalism to ensure co-operation between the parties.

Making Changes — Not

Don't make changes during the *implementation* phase of the contract. Spend sufficient time, initially, working on the contract and requirements specification so that the project does not need changes after the initial specification is set. If there is one behaviour that distinguishes professionals from amateurs, this is it. The objective should be *no changes* during implementation. They cost extra: even small changes can cause the vendor considerable disruption in the design effort, so the cost is almost always greater than you expect. If you *have* to make changes, then put them in writing using an agreed change procedure. I have worked with vendors who rely on changes to turn a profit, because initially they quoted low to obtain the contract.

Purchase Order or Contract?

When do you use a purchase order and when do you use a design-and-supply contract? Use a purchase order when the product or service you want is easy to describe and understand. These would be described in supplier's advertisements, brochures or catalogues. Some examples are: office stationery and equipment; office furniture, and services such as cleaning and routine building maintenance. You can also buy computer equipment that replaces equipment that you already own, because you are familiar with it — providing it does do not need extensive technical knowledge to set up. A purchase order is also suitable for the purchase of *limited* specialized professional services. You must concisely describe your requirements and expected outcomes on the face of the purchase order. This is a purchase order that is tending towards a simple contract. Examples of limited professional services are legal or technological advice on aspects of computer procurement such as: "search for a suitable specialized contract for the procurement of information technology equipment in the general retail business" and "research and compile independent reviews of software for a small manufacturing business".

On the back on your standard purchase order you will have 'General Terms and Conditions of Purchase'. These will give you adequate commercial protection for common purchases. If you do not have a standard purchase order for your business you can obtain a model, complete with the standard conditions, from professional purchasing organisations. The cost is low considering what you are getting in expertise. Look for an organisational name like 'Institute of Purchasing and Supply Management'. There is also an example 'Guide to General Terms and Conditions of Purchase' provided in Appendix A.

Use an information technology contract (which includes the requirement specification) when the equipment or service you want is technically complex, requires specialist engineering knowledge, and the purchase price if lost, would financially threaten the viability of your business. Unlike a purchase order, a contract is initially in draft form: you negotiate with your selected vendor until the final contract

31

is agreed between both parties and signed up. As a result each party has a clear idea of its responsibilities, and the legal implications are understood. The chapter *'Obtaining Your Specified Needs'* shows an example of a contract guide; the complexity of which is consistent with the commercial risks involved for a small to medium-size business. It is suitable for a commercial-off-the-shelf computer system only; a contract for the conceptual design and development of a computer system would require a far more complex contract, and is not the subject of this book.

Evaluating the Quotations

Evaluate the system features and characteristics contained in your quotations against the requirements specification. But also think about the organisational attributes that the vendors have displayed during your dealings with them. Did they listen? Did they explain how they work? Were they amenable to negotiation? Were they timely in response to your inquiries? Were they patient when you were seeking clarification. The vendor's behaviour can make an important contribution to the success of your project. When you are satisfied, make your choice.

Software Licenses

Software licenses can cost an astonishing amount of money when there are multiple users. There are a number of different types depending upon the software suppliers who issue them. Examples are: per user license, workstation license, concurrent user license, network license, site license and enterprise license. Each license is a complex legal document and the large software suppliers are forever devising new ways of increasing their profitability though new forms of licensing. To give yourself some measure of protection, do the costing and obtain professional legal advice for the interpretation of the license that you propose to use.

A means of reducing software licensing costs is to consider using software developed by supporters of the General Public License (GPL). In practice this means software developed by the GNU/Linux community, although there are other types of Free Software licenses they are not so well known. This software is free of direct licensing costs and is also cost-free or low-cost to purchase. The specialized vendors who deal in GLP software will charge for their engineering expertise, software packaging, installation, support and maintenance services the same as any other vendor, but your long-term subscription costs can be a fraction of the cost of proprietary licenses.

Guidance. [I use the qualifier 'fraction' of the cost, because there is more than one General Public License, and not all of them are completely free of copyright or cost. There are around fifty of what are genetically called **'open-source licenses'** *and these vary in the way they can be used, and the way in which license fees (if any) are calculated. Open-source software is widely used on Internet servers, thin client LANs,* *embedded into mobile phones and personal digital assistants, often without the user being aware that they are using it. In the past, the scientific community and the technically adventurous used open-source software because of its superior stability, robustness and relative freedom from malicious attack. Today it has developed to the point where its ease of use equals that of proprietary software, and it is being steadily adopted by government organisations, businesses and individuals who want to keep their information management costs down. There are vendors who specialize in the migration from proprietary to open-source software, and those who integrate open-source software into existing proprietary software systems.]*

Telecommunications Contracts

To connect your LAN to other organisation's WANs, the Internet and any of your business mobile users, you will need to complete separate user contracts with various telecommunication service providers. Since these organisations are usually selling to the World, they have rigid service contracts. There is not much you can do about this, except shop around and look for the most suitable to meet your needs. If you are a heavy user, or part of a larger organisation you may, by negotiation, obtain a favourable contract due to the effect of market forces. Otherwise you have to take what is on offer.

Useful Network Knowledge

This chapter describes general network characteristics at a low technical level. Its purpose is to assist you to write the Requirements Specification (explained in the chapter *'Writing the Requirements Specification'*) to send to vendors with the request for a quotation.

Guidance. *[In this book the descriptions 'network' and 'computer system' generally mean the same. If I am describing the nature in which the computers are connected up, then I use the word network, as in this chapter; if I am describing the whole facility in a general way, I use the term computer system. If I am inconsistent, forgive me — you'll know what I mean.]*

There are different kinds of networks. Computers which are close to one another, such as in the same room or building, are described as being connected with a Local Area Network (LAN). Computers which are distant from one another, such as in other cities or countries, are described as being connected with a Wide Area Network (WAN) or Internet. A LAN and WAN are private, the Internet is public.

Elaborating upon these distinctions. A business LAN is a private network: you specify, own, maintain, and choose the content and who will use it. A business WAN is also a private network, but in a different way. Because of the distant locations between, say, branch offices of the business, you use a telecommunications company to provide you with the required infrastructure and technical services. You pay a regular subscription for these, after signing a contract defining the type of network services to be provided. Only your business's information travels over this WAN: the public do not have access to it, even though it may use common telecommunications infrastructure which also carries public services.

Private networks have other names. LANs are called intranets (within the walls of an enterprise); some types of WANs are called extranets (outside the walls of an enterprise): these are when the enterprise allows other organisations to access the WAN with permission. Examples are business suppliers, consultants and clients.

The Internet is a global communications network consisting of numerous separately owned telecommunications networks. There is no central control over the content or access to the Internet: therefore it is *public space*. The World Wide Web is a means of broadcasting various types of content on the Internet and most of this content is also public.

You can use the Internet as part of your private network by employing specialized techniques known as tunnelling. You pay a telecommunications service provider to set-up this service when you require it. Generally this book talks about private computer networks.

Principal Network Types

There are two distinct network types: client-server and peer-to-peer. They could look the same from the outside using common hardware parts and physical connection, but the notable difference is in the location of information, the software applications and stored data. In a pure client-server network all the information is centralized — it resides on the server; and in a pure peer-to-peer network all the information is distributed — it is stored   across the network on the workstations. In practice, the distinction between them is not so clear cut. If a server runs, say, an email service, it will have some of this application and its data stored on the workstations; and if a peer-to-peer network provides a database, it will run the database on one workstation, which for this application acts like a server. The distinction between the network types is easier to see in small networks, as larger more complex networks use a combination of both, such as client-server networks in branch offices connected together in a peer-to-peer chain. The peer-to-peer chain may run on a private network or a public network such as the Internet.

In extensive high integrity networks such as those deployed by large organisations there is a third type of network consisting of distributed servers connected together. Here the servers are typically in clusters to provide high reliability, with a number of clusters geographically dispersed throughout the network to provide operational redundancy and data backup. In other words, such a network can continue in service with the breakdown of some servers and the loss of part of the network. A national business information database on the Internet will be of this type, so I mention it so that when you are connecting to it, you will understand what you are dealing with. I am not going into detail about this type of network

The network type is determined by the combination of hardware and software chosen to make up the parts of the network. This choice forms a particular physical and logical architecture that determines the way in which information is controlled and directed in the network. You need not be too concerned about the technicalities; the vendor will do the technical design. Choosing between the two distinct types of network will depend not so much on technical considerations, but more on how you wish to manage and use the network. Each network type has its advantages and disadvantages.

Client-Server Network

The advantages of a client-server network are:

- They are flexible in operation, so that it's easy to extend the network by adding equipment and reconfiguring the network to accommodate the changes required by the addition of new users. And vice versa for removing users.

- There is a wide range of compatible software available, so that you can add new services for network users with standard off-the-shelf software applications.

- There is extensive industrial information available about servers compared to peer-to-peer. This makes problem-solving less difficult for the network administrator and end-user.

- The administration of the network is centralised on the server and under control of one trained person.

- The network can be made secure against unauthorised access compared to a peer-to-peer network.

The disadvantages of client-server are:

- For a small number of users, say two or three, they are more expensive per user connection compared to a peer-to-peer network, but with the falling prices of small business servers it would be worth the effort of pricing a server and diskless workstations even for a small number of workstations. See the next sub-heading.

- They require more technical knowledge, experience and skill to set up and run than required for a peer-to-peer network.

- Generally a breakdown of the server brings down all the workstations (so fault-tolerance is an essential characteristic of servers).

In business, meeting the regulations governing your industry can only be done with a client-server network; the peer-to-peer network described later is unable to meet the data security standards demanded by the regulatory authorities. In addition, businesses require a workstation and its network to act as an effective tool to assist in the delivery of user and customer services. Users and customers do not want to get involved in the day-to-day administration of the network, since they are unlikely to have the time or the inclination for this activity. Therefore the feature of central administration offered by a client-server network is attractive to businesses, as the control of the network is in the hands of one person. The data security and the central administration features of the client-server network make it the natural choice for professional use. In general, this book deals with the client-server network type.

Diskless Workstations

The client-server network enables you to take advantage of the possibility of diskless workstations (where there are no hard disk drives or removable disk drives at the workstations). This is the client-server network in its purest practical form, with all the software applications and data residing on the server (except for communication services and the user workstation display applications). There are no facilities at the workstations for manually loading applications or data and therefore no chance of users interfering with the network's configuration. Diskless workstations are also known as thin-clients, thin-stations or diskless nodes on a network. I will use the term thin-client as it is in widespread use. To differentiate, a workstation *with* disks is called a thick-client. The advantages of the thin-client network are:

- The cost of each workstation is lower than that of a standard thick-client personal computer. The more thin-clients you have on a network the greater the overall saving on workstations. The greatest cost savings are with a limited suite of software delivered to a large number of users on the network.

- You can achieve and demonstrate a high standard of network security as users cannot interfere with the network. If you have wireless thin-client portables deployed within the LAN or roving within an external WAN and any are lost through stealing, then the business data is safe as it all resides on the server. Replacing the portables is not as disruptive to the business as losing sensitive data to unknown persons.

- The network administrator can upgrade or update each thin-client's software from a central server without visiting and updating each workstation. So the network administration costs are lower for thin-clients than for thick-clients.

- There is less user training and supervision required regarding network security compared to users of the standard thick-client workstation.

- They have easier workstation failure management, as a thin-client can be replaced directly with another thin-client with minimal disruption to the user.

- They have less energy consumption than the equivalent number or thick-clients.

- The thin-client workstations are more reliable than thick-client workstations, because they are less complex, run cooler, are fanless, and so develop faults less frequently.

- They are ideal for hostile industrial environments where the displays are sealed units with touch screen inputs.

- Upgrades of the workstations are less frequent; display units, keyboards and pointing devices do not require upgrading to use the latest software applications. Software and hardware upgrades are done at the server.

- Less attractive to most thieves. They have to steal the entire system to have a chance of disposing the equipment profitably.

- They are usually aesthetically pleasing and take up little desktop space.

The disadvantages are:

- The network server needs to be more powerful than a thick-client server, so that it can run all the shared applications as well as other server tasks such as file storage and communication services; or you may need more than one server for a given number of clients. This increases the server cost (but not necessarily the overall system cost, due to the savings made at the workstations).

- It is inflexible; each user can access only a defined suite of applications software. If you have a user who requires specialised applications software not required by others, you need to provide that user with a standard thick-client workstation. In this case the user, to some extent, owns the specialised software on their workstation and look after it themselves.

- The greatest cost savings are when the computer peripherals of printers and scanners are shared between users on the network. This causes some inconvenience to the users, as sometimes they have to wait to access a required service.

- If the server (assuming one server) malfunctions, all client computing ceases and the system is unusable.

Peer-To-Peer Network

Peer-to-peer type networks have their uses. In a home or small office where the data security and network administration requirements are not stringent, they provide an inexpensive and simple method of networking computers. You can share files and other resources such as printers, scanners and Internet access. Most common computer operating systems have peer-to-peer networking facilities built-in as a standard product feature. In addition to small local peer-to-peer networks there are large specialised peer-to-peer networks on the Internet which provide a single service, such as music sharing, to large numbers of users; but we are not talking about this type of peer-to-peer network here.

The advantages of a peer-to-peer network are:

- The network does not require a dedicated server to run the network.

- It's possible, in small numbers, to connect existing workstations together to share resources easily. Also, if you have wireless workstations or portables, then you can connect the computers together in an 'ad hoc' peer-to-peer group. Here you can exchange information freely, so long as you are a member of the group. These groups can be conveniently formed or disbanded as required.

- It's technically easier to operate than a client-server network, but has to be administered though the workstation users. This causes problems if users aren't disciplined in their workstation administration.

- If communication between workstations fails, each one reverts to a stand-alone computer and continues operating (most of the time depending upon the nature of the fault).

The disadvantages of a peer-to-peer are:

- It's not as flexible regarding network expansion as a client-server network. There is a limit on the total number of users, which is determined by the network operating system employed. This total number of users is small compared to the total number of users possible with client-server.

- The administration of each workstation is in the hands of the workstation user.

- It is difficult to make the network secure compared to client-server.

- All the workstations have to be operational for each user to share all of the other user's network files and resources.

Network Physical Connections

Although the different types and sizes of businesses have different network connection needs, there are only two basic types of network connections in *widespread* use. These are the Bus and the Star. A small business network can look like a bus or a star, while a much larger network may, because of its complexity, be difficult to identify as one of these basic types, but will be made up of a combinations of them. In buildings where it is difficult to lay cables you can use wireless networks which get around the problem of having to make a physical connections between different parts of the network. As well as the physical connection, the *logical* connection of computers on a network refers to the logical relationship between computers used to direct information through the physical network. The heading *'Network Logical Connections'* later explains more about this.

Bus Connection

Figure 2, A Bus Physical Connection, shows the main parts. In this type of network the workstations and server are connected together in the form of a chain. This connection is also known by the quaint name of a daisy-chain. The daisy heads representing the computers and the stems the wiring. The advantage of bus connection is its simplicity and effective use of wiring. It uses less wiring than the star connection (described below) provided that the workstations are more or less lined up on the same building floor level, and there is no wiring required between upper and lower floors. Therefore the main use of bus topology is in small networks where the computers are located close to one another.

Star Connection

Figure 3, A Star Physical Connection, shows the main parts. This connection has the advantage of flexibility and expandability. It is easier than other connections to deal with awkward wiring runs presented by problematic building layouts on several floors. Its vulnerability is that if the hub or switch (in the centre) develops a fault then the whole network becomes inoperative; but if it happens the cause of the fault becomes obvious by easy substitution of network equipment. The star connection uses greater lengths of network cabling compared to the bus connection in situations where the computers are close to one another on the same level.

If the centre of the star network is a hub, it can be of two sorts: a passive hub or an active hub. A passive hub provides a central location to physically and electrically connect the parts of the network together, it does nothing more so does not require a power supply (a passive hub is a useful device for fault finding). An active hub, which requires a power supply, does the same as a passive hub and provides one or more active functions, the most common being providing repeaters for the connection ports. If a hub provides repeaters then the outgoing star cables can have a longer reach to the workstations and server, which further assists in the solving of wiring problems. If the centre of the star network is a *switch*, which is a sophisticated active hub, it provides additional network management functions that enhance the performance of the network. Because of this switches have almost completely superseded hubs as the centre of a star network. There are other types of network physical connections such as clustered star, ring, tree and mesh, but the star connection is so common that I will use it in the network examples in this book.

Network Logical Connections

The logical connection of a network describes the logical relationship between computers used to direct information through the physical network in a defined way.

41

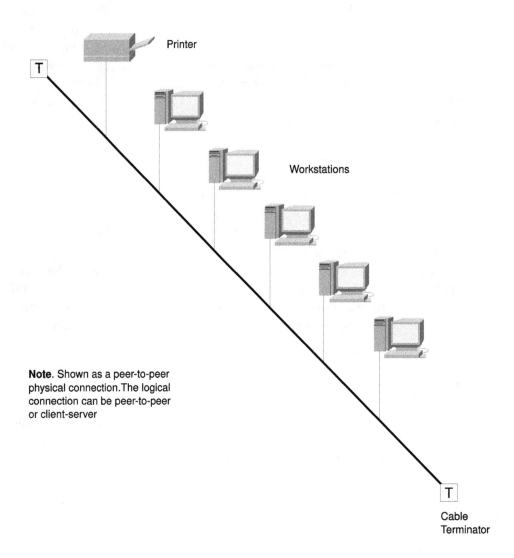

Figure 2: A Bus Physical Connection

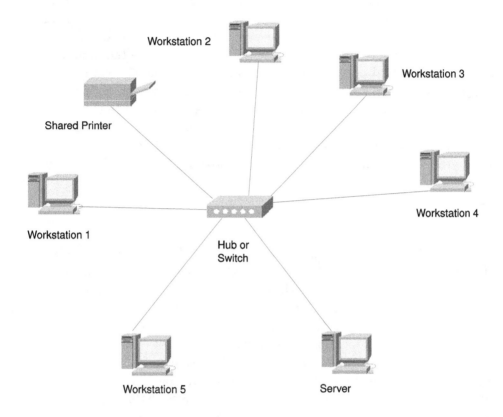

Note. Shown as a client-server physical and
logical network. Each workstation or server
can have its own peripherals
(Not shown for clarity)

Figure 3: A Star Physical Connection

In other words, the manner in which information is transmitted between one connection and another. It's not the way a network looks. The two common logical connections, as in physical connections, are peer-to-peer and client-server. In a peer-to-peer network the workstations talk directly to one another, because the data and the applications providing network services are distributed across the network. In a client-server network the workstations do not talk directly to one another (although they are able to do so) but though the server (or servers). Because that's where all the data is, and that's where the applications which provide the network services are held. Each logical connection can run on either of the physical connections of bus or star. As with network physical connections there are other types of network logical connections, such as clustered star, ring, tree and mesh. In the requirements specification you specify which network services (business or office software applications, email, and Internet access for instance) you need at each workstation; the network designer has the task of choosing the logical and physical topology.

Databases

A database is an electronic filing system that is capable of holding a large amount and variety of information. It can hold text, drawings, illustrations, charts and photographic images, and it forms the core of an information management system. The database filing system holds the information in the form of electronic 'cards' called records; each record contains fields through which you enter and store data. The electronic cards are analogous to physical cards with the information handwritten or typed on them in a manual card filing system. Because of its electronic nature a database has additional management functions not found in a manual card filing system. These are the ability to relate records to one another and as a result search for particular records or multiple records using simple or complex search criteria. The search process is called querying the database. An example of a simple query is a search using a customers name to find their record, and an example of a complex query is a search for how many customers had a particular product or service during a specified period of time, in a given geographical area. The ability to run complex queries makes the database a powerful tool in the analysis of information.

To maintain their usefulness databases have to be kept up to date. Customer's personal details and needs change over time as they experience altered circumstances. These changes have to be recorded in a timely manner. If not, the database becomes a less and less useful information management tool, and if neglected for a long period becomes useless. Database users have to take responsibility for entering changes into the database as the changes occur: this prevents the information held in the database becoming outdated.

This problem of information changing over time causes a further difficulty. If two or more databases are set up to hold some common information, in practice they will be separately updated in a slightly different manner. No matter how disciplined your approach — over time the common information that is supposed to be the same becomes different! Good information management requires one set of data to reside in a master database which, through electronic links, transfers the data automatically to slave databases in other locations. When the master database is updated the changes are passed on to the slave databases, so that the contents of common record fields are congruent in all respects. Another advantage of this method is that the changing data is only entered once which results in a useful productivity gain.

The user graphical interface of the database application program determines the method of entry of data into the database. But generally the editable data is entered through labelled fields and use of the computer keyboard. In addition, with the appropriate software, it is possible to enter editable data though a scanner, a handwriting tablet or through voice. For storing images, professional grade scanners can handle editable data and images in various forms, or you can use the database application's import function. A database can run on a workstation or a server depending upon the configuration of the network; large databases run on a server so that the full database functionality can be realised though the extra computing power of the server.

Apart from the obvious use of electronic customer records, databases are commonly embedded into other software applications such as sales order processing software. Link common data together if you have two or more separate databases. If you are intending to scan electronic customer records you will need the bridging or interface software between the scanner application and the database proper. This is needed to translate the scanner data format into the database data format. Specify this bridging software in the requirements specification by stating that the database needs to communicate with, and capture data from, your other specified software applications.

Mobile Computing

Mobile computers form part of the physical and logical connections of the network. They include Laptops, Tablet PCs, Net-books, Ultra-Portables and the smaller handhelds that are marketed under names such as Personal Digital Assistants (PDAs), Pocket PCs, and Smart Phones. The expensive high-end laptops can have the computing power comparable to the average desktop computer. Mobile computers can communicate securely with the office network though the Internet over the public telecommunications system, whether by land-line, mobile telephone network, or communications satellite. Specify them as an integral part of the office network, in particular, make arrangements to ensure that their data content is backed-up with the rest of the data on the office network. There is a wide range of business software existing for mobile computers; use the same research methods to find something suitable, just as you do for the main office software. For more information look under the heading *'Needs Analysis'* in the chapter *'Management Issues and How to Get Started'*.

Network Security

A top computer company sets up an experiment to measure the number of attacks an unprotected off-the-shelf server would suffer on the Internet. The experiment lasts five days. In the first fifteen minutes there were twenty random attacks. During the course of the next five days there were four hundred random attacks consisting of anonymous attackers trying find security vulnerabilities in the server. Without analysing the results here, the point of presenting these figures is to illustrate that securing your business network is not a theoretical issue, but one of practical importance in protecting your business information. The objectives of common attacks on business networks are:

- Denial of Service Attacks that deprive the legitimate user of the services offered by the system.

- Steal secrets, such as commercial, financial and technological information.

- Invade and control your machines without your knowledge and use them for illegal activities such as Distributed Denial of Service Attacks on other people's servers.

- Nuisance attacks, injecting destructive viruses, by knowledgeable non-professionals for self gratification or infamy.

Now the amount of time and money spent on defending — *and* crackers attacking — your business network, depends upon the value of the information contained on your servers. The higher the value of business information you own, the more resources and time a cracker will employ to steal that information, but even low value business information need *some* protection. Nuisance attacks can disrupt your business and cause loss of income, even if the cracker does not obtain anything of value in the way of information. Unless you are a security expert, you have to leave the decision concerning the degree of protection for your business to the vendor, who has the expertise to match the level of protection to the level of risk for your type of business. Choose, if possible, a vendor who has experience in your business or industrial sector. Many large vendors have divisions which deal with the major business sectors such as aerospace, primary industry, medical, finance, manufacturing, construction and retail.

The network examples in Figure 4, Figure 5 and Figure 6 show physical firewalls as a means of protection against external malicious intrusion. This is one technique used with other methods to secure a network. Some other methods are password protection, user authentication, limiting services to users, encrypting data, intrusion detection systems, network separation and the creation of virtual private networks.

Network Examples

To help you devise your network specification, Figure 4, Figure 5 and Figure 6 show network layouts providing services required by typical businesses. They show general physical networks so that you can see the characteristics of business networks. The installed hardware of a business network will differ from the representations in the figures because there are many different ways of implementing the same network functions. For instance, the firewalls are often integrated into functional units such as modems/routers/gateways, or the two firewalls 'Frontend Firewall' and 'Backend Firewall', are integrated into a single unit called a triple port, triple interface or three legged firewall.

Security professionals use the terms External Zone, Internal Zone and Demilitarized Zone (DMZ) to denote the different levels of risk present in a typical network. The External Zone denotes the highest risk, such as the Internet or a wireless network. The Internal Zone denotes the lowest risk, such as a private network behind a firewall. The Demilitarized Zone denotes an intermediate risk limited network, usually used to protect a private network from a connected Internet server which is likely to be attacked from time to time.

Wired LAN

You need to be aware of the reason for these extra firewalls in Figure 5 and Figure 6. The security precautions needed when a business server is delivering services through the Internet to customers are more stringent than a server delivering services to private LAN users. So the Internet servers are placed in the Demilitarized Zone (DMZ). In this zone the Internet servers are partially protected (hence DMZ) from malicious attacks from the Internet by the front-end firewall. They cannot be made more secure because the services they provide give malicious attackers (crackers) the means of entry for an intrusion. To take account of this, Internet servers are hardened to increase their resistance to malicious attack. In contrast, the local servers are protected by an additional back-end firewall giving them improved protection from external intrusion, so the security precautions required for them are less stringent. If the Internet server is compromised then the LAN still has the added protection of the back-end firewall keep it secure.

Wireless LAN

In Figure 6, the Wireless LAN Firewall protects the wired LAN from malicious intrusion from the wireless portion of the network (sub-network). Wireless LANs are more vulnerable to malicious intrusion than wired LANs because anyone with a laptop computer can access the Wireless LAN radio transmission and attack it at their leisure. The legitimate laptops which are part of the business wireless network will have software firewalls installed on them (not shown), to protect them from possible malicious intrusion. This is because a wireless cracker can attack both the wireless LAN or the local roaming laptops.

Information and Data Standards

All businesses exchange and share information with customers, other businesses, and various other organisations. In the computing world, standards institutions generate standards designed to facilitate the exchange of computer information and the storage of data. The idea is that unrelated applications will be able to exchange data with one another, so making it possible to integrate dissimilar vendors products in one system. The advantage of standards is that you are not locked in to the products of a single vendor. You can choose applications that best suit your needs, and they will work together on the network though standard interfaces to and from standard storage formats. An illustration of the financial value of standardisation to the user becomes visible when you replace an application that contains electronic customer records. Say, after many years of use, you have all the customer's information electronically stored on a database which has reached its data capacity limit. Now, if you want to increase the capacity of the database because your customer base is increasing, you need to transfer all of that customer data into replacement software. With standardisation you can do this inexpensively by transferring the data electronically; instead of using the expensive alternative of physically keying in all the data though the keyboard.

One example of a widely adopted standard is the Portable Document Format (PDF), which, although being a commercial product, has become one of the de facto standards for the transmission of electronic documents. Another is the non-commercial Open Document Format (ODF) which is a document file format for the sharing of electronic office documents, such as word processing, spreadsheets, charts and presentations. Many software suppliers, both commercial and non-commercial are incorporating this file standard into their office applications software. The ODF is particularly suitable for organisations such as governments, which need to give public access to documents without bias towards a particular software supplier. Since its adoption as an international standard (ISO/IEC 26300) it is also useful to organisations which have a public responsibility for maintaining data access for long historical periods (hundreds of years).

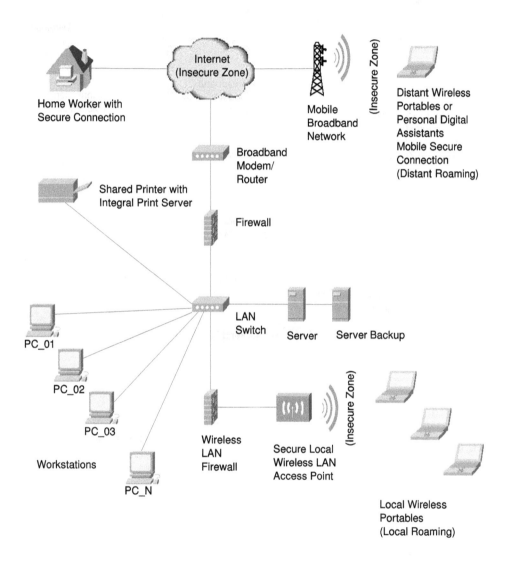

Figure 4: A General Business Network

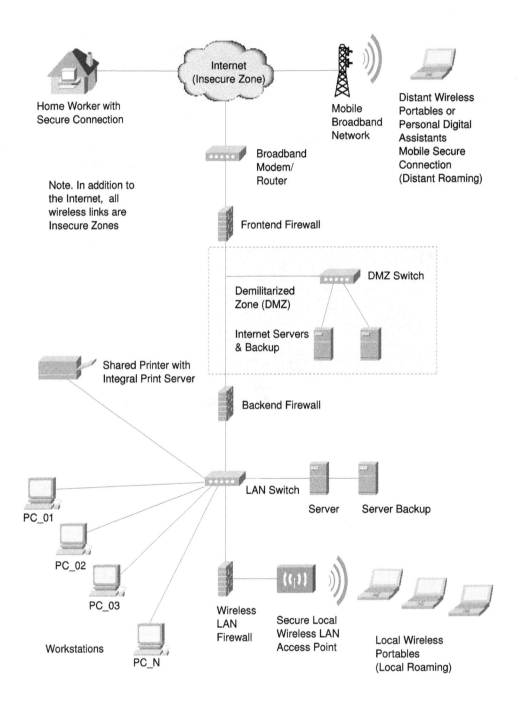

Figure 5: An Internet Service Network

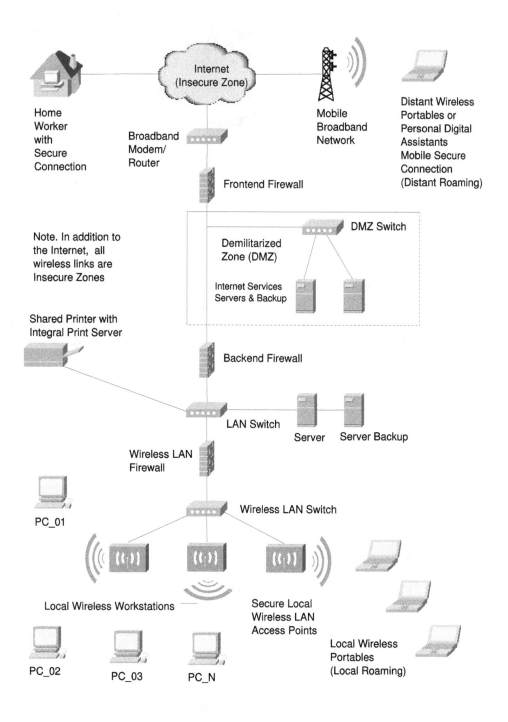

Figure 6: A Wireless and Internet Network

If your business delivers documents to customers through the Internet then the widespread standard format for doing this is PDF. This is because the PDF reader is available free to anyone for installation in a wide variety of operating systems, so all customers can read your documents with ease.

Convergence of Digital Services

Before personal computers became widespread commodity products, we had our communication and entertainment services delivered separately. Telephone companies provided our telephone services; broadcasting companies provided radio and television programmes; music production companies delivered music recorded on disks playable on home equipment; and film production companies distributed films to our local cinemas. The underlying technologies of these information delivery systems were different from one another, and therefore could not be combined and delivered as a single integrated information service to the consumer (business or domestic). The development of the personal computer brought about the realization that almost all electronic signals could be digitized, and with international technical effort, they could be standardized and used worldwide. In time, this led to the idea of convergence.

Convergence is the delivery of different types of information services to a single customer access point. Examples of access points are personal computers; mobile phones; home television and music centres; personal digital assistants (PDAs) and public information booths. Not all access points deliver the same range of information content, and the delivery quality varies depending upon the nature of the telecommunications infrastructure providing the service.

What has all this to do with networked computers in business? Well, in business you need a range of information services to run your business successfully. A Local Area Network can capture a wide range of information services in addition to the local computer information in your office. Because of converging technologies data-only networks developed into data and voice networks (telephone and facsimile), and in turn, these turned into data, voice and video networks (television-like pictures). So you can have everything together. The most likely information needs of a modern business are for computer data networks; telephone services, both fixed and mobile; and video-conferencing.

In addition to *receiving* information, your business may need to *deliver* information to its customers. It can do this by means of the LAN and the Internet combined. You will need a server on the Internet, which, not protected by the LAN firewall, will need additional security measures to protect it against malicious attack.

It is economical to include these additional services into your computer LAN when you are specifying your computer system. You may not want to include all the additional services into the computer system at once, but it is wise to specify that

File Size Range	Type of Data Contained in the File
1- 100 Kilobytes	Plain text and email (Word-processing)
10 – 2000 Kilobytes	Still graphics (line diagrams and clip art)
1 – 5 Megabytes	Audio (speech, fragments of music)
5 – 10 Megabytes	Still video (photographic images)
1 – 100 Megabytes	Combined text, graphics, audio and video
1 – 3 Gigabytes	Software installations
3 – 50 Gigabytes	Complete HDD images (operating system and applications)

Table 1: File Size Ranges

the system is expandable in the future to include these without disruption of your existing LAN.

One problem for non-technical people is learning the jargon associated with these additional technologies. At times it seems overwhelming; and leaving the task entirely to the vendor appears to be the ideal solution. Don't do it! Because you use exactly the same management process to deal with all technology purchases. Knowing this, cuts the problem down to a manageable size. You specify what you want in terms of *user* functionality, and let the vendor demonstrate that they can meet your requirements. Although the details will be different for each technology, follow the same process as described in this book for the implementation of computer networks. There is more information on this subject in the chapter *'Management Issues and How to Get Started'* under the subheading *'Dealing with the System Vendor'*.

Network Performance

Network performance means the speed at which data travels though the network from one computer to another. High speed means high performance. The larger the data file the more data you have to transfer from the source computer to the destination computer in a given time; so, if you have large files you will need a fast network if you don't want to wait long for the information to arrive. If you have small files a slower network will do. Since high speed networks cost more than low speed networks, you estimate the required performance from a knowledge of the average file size used on your workstations, and an acceptable time for the transfer of these files across the network. Table 1, shows typical file sizes against common computer file types. From these you can estimate the average file sizes that you are likely to generate at the various workstations.

For a more reliable estimate of files sizes, note the sizes of your stand-alone computer files and calculate their average. If you don't have any computers yet, then visit a computerised business similar in nature to yours, and gain the information you need from them.

To give you a feel for the time taken to transfer files across the network from one workstation to another, or from a server to a workstation, here is an example calculation of transfer time. Before we start, you need to know that network speeds are specified at data rates of 1, 2, 10, and 100 Megabits per second. As technology advances these speeds will rise; 1 Gigabits per second will soon be commonplace, with 10 Gigabits per second following close behind. One hundred Megabits per second LANs are common and affordable, so we will use this speed in our calculation. There are eight bits in every byte, so this conversion appears in the calculation.

Example:

Taking a file size of 1 to 100 MegaBytes and a LAN data rate of 100 Megabits per second we have transfer times of the range:

Transfer time in seconds $= \frac{filesize(MB) \times 8}{network\,data\,rate(Mbps)}$

Transfer time for low end of file size $= \frac{1MB \times 8}{100Mbps} = 0.08$ seconds

Transfer time for high end of file size $= \frac{100MB \times 8}{100Mbps} = 8.0$ seconds

As a rule of thumb networks are reckoned to operate at 80 per cent of maximum theoretical speed, so the above figures become longer to 0.1 secs and 10 secs. In addition this calculation is for one user: assuming that the network is not busy with other users. When you have concurrent users, the network speed drops further depending upon the size of the additional traffic load. So a second rule of thumb is that a busy network can fall to between one-third and two-thirds of the theoretical speed. These considerations are for the network designer to ponder: they have traffic loading formulae for working out the required network speed. What you do is state the user requirements in terms of file size and acceptable transfer time.

Data Backup and System Recovery

"Eighty percent of companies without well-conceived data protection and recovery strategies go out of business within two years of a major disaster". Source: United States Archives and Records Administration. Notice that this statement includes the word recovery, because you need to be competent at information backup *and* recovery in equal measure. Without analysing the details of this statement, the message is clear: if you depend on computers to run your business, then its long-term survival will depend upon you safeguarding your business information.

Computer data is vulnerable. A mistake by an inexperienced user, a virus infection, a malicious attack, a lightning strike, a power supply transient or failure, an operating system crash, a hard disk drive (HDD) failure or other hardware component failure can cause the partial or complete loss of working data.

The vulnerability of computer data is reduced to an acceptable level by copying the business data residing on the working HDD on to removable media. This stores the data in a much safer way than storage on the working media alone. The copying process is called backing-up and the copied data the backup data. If working data is lost or corrupted, then it is restored from the backup media by a data recovery process. In most systems, application software called (naturally) backup software, controls both the back-up and, when needed, the recovery process.

There are two types of information backup — business data backup only (such as word processing or spreadsheet files on the HDD file system), and computer system data (the entire HDD data image) backup. Business data backup is the preservation of your business information for later restoration — *provided that the computer system is still operational*. System data backup is the preservation of the entire hard drive image for later restoration — *when the computer system has crashed and is non-operational*. Because the computer system is non-operational, this process is called bare-metal recovery or HDD image recovery. First, in the paragraphs below, we are going to talk about business data restoration, and then talk about system recovery later in this chapter. For brevity, and because the terms are in general use, sometimes we will call business data backup 'data backup', and system data backup, 'system backup'.

Generally backup software is reliable, but if there is a malfunction with the backup software or with writing the data to the removable media, the backup software will, in most cases, display an error message. So that you know, in this case, that the data on the removable media is corrupted or missing, and you can correct the malfunction and repeat the operation.

Because backing-up takes time, some businesses which cannot afford to be out of touch with their customers at all, such as Internet service providers, use the sophisticated method of automatic changeover from a failed server to an identical stand-by server. The change-over is so quick, that customers don't notice that anything is amiss.

Data Backup — Media Sets

To guard against damage to the backup media, you have *sets* of removable media. Each member of the set (each item of removable medium: tape, disk, flash drive or not-yet-invented) is rotated in a particular sequence, so the saved data is *distributed* across a number of backup media. There is an example of a backup media rotation sequence in the chapter *'Managing Normal Operation'*. One set of backup media, included in the rotation, is moved to a *separate location* for safe-keeping. If you do not want to transport it, you can arrange the separation by transmitting the data to a distant Internet site backup facility. These facilities are professional backup services for which you pay an annual subscription.

Guidance. *[The two characteristics mentioned above (data distributed through or across a media set, and the rolling or sequential geographical separation of one of the media sets), give secure backup at reasonable cost. There are shiny, high-tech, high-capacity backup products on the market at attractive prices, which do not meet these essential requirements. These products do not store your data as safely as it could be — be aware.]*

Having sets of removable media also has the advantage of avoiding the lengthy process of doing a full data backup every day. You can use Incremental or Differential backup each day, with a full backup once a working week. This saves you a lot of time. The next section explains Incremental and Differential backup, and the way that you use it in practice is explained in the chapter *'Managing Normal Operation'*.

To guard against the cases where there is a backup malfunction, but no error message displayed, backup applications have a backup verify function. This compares the backed-up data to the working data and detects any difference. The backup application displays an error message if there is any difference (there shouldn't be).

Which Data

Deciding which data to back-up is an exercise in risk management, can you risk losing some data, all data, or no data? Data, such as email and databases are awkward to back up and restore. So when you specify the backup application mention that you need these backing up in particular, if that is the case.

The disadvantage of backing up the data files *only*, is that if you have a system crash, its restoration is time-consuming. This is because you have to separately reload the operating system; all the applications, their upgrades, the application's configuration parameters, and your personal preferences. This exercise can represent many days work, and perhaps a few weeks work with larger systems. It is a long time to be off-line, and unable to do business in the normal way. The advantage data files only, is that the required capacity of the removable media is smaller compared with full system recovery backup, making it less expensive.

If you want to bring your computer system quickly on-line after a system crash, then use a full system recovery backup application. See the section *'System Recovery'* in this chapter for more detail of these applications.

How Often

According to the value of the data to your business you decide on the quantity of data to be backed up, and also the frequency at which this process takes place. Clearly, all data that is classified as valuable will be selected for backing up. The question of frequency is answered by judging how much data loss your business could tolerate. For instance, if it was one days' worth, then it would be acceptable to back-up once every twenty-four hours. This is a common solution, with the backup process taking place outside office hours. In a second instance, you may judge that you could not afford to lose more than one hours' data without compromising the business; in this case the backup process would be scheduled to take place every hour during the working day.

If the data being currently entered by the users has immediate value and is critical to your business, then you have to adopt what is known as real-time backup. This promptly saves all the data that changes during a user session and offers backup throughout the working day. It is more complex and expensive than the scheduled backup method mentioned above. This degree of data security is not widespread, but the decision to adopt it is, again, one of risk assessment.

In a network, the working data resides on a server in the client-server model, or is distributed on the workstations in the peer-to-peer model. In some networks there is a combination of data on the server and on the workstations. The backup and restoration software collects the data from various sources and moves it to the target backup media. The backup media could be a separate connection on the network or integrated into the server. Either way, the process of backing up generates network traffic. There are number of backup processes which reduce the volume of data that is moved at any one time during backup. Knowing these processes, explained below, will enable you to specify the backup features required for your system. For a widely accepted routine backup process see the chapter *'Managing Normal Operation'*, under the heading *'A Backup Method'*.

Other Backup Characteristics

For information on how to specify the backup media capacity, the backup time and the backup equipment, see under the heading *'Defining Data Backup and System Recovery'* in the chapter *'Writing the Requirements Specification'*.

Backup Process

Computer data is contained in files. Typically, there are many files, and each one is a wrapping which encapsulates a particular set of data. Files have external attributes that define how the file will be handled by the computer. One of the attributes tells the computer, through the backup application software, that a file has been recently backed up, and the backup data is identical to the working data. So, the computer knows that the file does not need further backing up unless the contents are changed once again by the user. So, if the user does not access the file again, it is not saved at the next backup session, but remains archived (unchanged) on the backup media.

Data Full Backup (All Selected Files)

This process feature allows the systems administrator to select all the files that require backing up at one session. On completion of the backup process, all the selected files are backed up. These files will not be backed up at the next session unless they are changed or reselected. The purpose of this feature is to ensure that all selected files are represented and up to date in the backup medium set. In business, the systems administrator carries out a full backup at prescribed intervals (typically weekly) and uses either incremental or differential backup each day between the prescribed intervals.

Incremental Backup

This feature backs up all selected files that are new or changed since the last incremental or full backup.

Differential Backup

This feature backs up all the selected files that are new or changed since the last full backup.

Making the Choice

Full data backup is always needed; the choice between differential and incremental backup is based on the time it takes to back up versus the time it takes to restore. In a reliable network, restoring files is an infrequent occurrence, so the time to back up is of greater consequence since it occurs every working day. Table 2, Backup Types, summarises the relative characteristics to help you decide.

Incremental and differential methods reduce the amount network traffic generated during the backup process; this is only important if you are backing up during the working day. If you are backing up outside office hours where the additional amount of network traffic is not important, you can use full backup without slowing the network down for other users. In this situation, incremental and differential backup simply saves operator's time during the backup process.

Type of Backup	Data files that will be backed up	Relative time for backup	Relative time to restore
Full	All selected files regardless of when they were previously backed up.	High	Low
Incremental	Selected new and changed files since the last incremental or full backup.	Low	High: because of multiple backup media.
Differential	Selected new and changed files since the last full backup.	Moderate	Moderate: only two backup media required.

Table 2: Backup Types

Testing the Data Backup System

Part of your data backup schedule should include a restoration test of the backup software application. With data backup alone, as compared to system recovery, the process is straightforward. Add a new data folder to the working file system called something like 'BackUpTest'. Start the backup application, then transfer some backed up folders or files from the backup medium to the working medium (your working hard drive). Check that the restored files work as expected.

Restoring Data Files

You restore lost working files from sets of backup medium. A set consists of the medium employed for a full data backup together with the medium employed for the incremental or differential backup since the last full data backup. The number of working files requiring restoration depends upon whether you have experienced a complete or partial loss of data on the network. The backup software allows you to select the files on the removable media that need restoration and direct them to the working files on the hard disk drive. When this process is complete you can resume normal network operation.

What Happens Between Backups?

Computer consultancies carrying out poll studies amongst information managers have produced a useful insight about the common causes of data loss between backups. The exact numbers are variable, depending upon the nature of the pollster's

Common Causes of Data Loss	Percentage of Total
Computer Viruses	7%
Natural Disasters	3%
Hardware System Malfunction	44%
Operator Human Error	32%
Software Malfunction	14%

Table 3: Common Causes of Data Loss

questionnaire and the industrial sector polled. Here is one set of figures in Table 3, Common Causes of Data Loss.

These results may not be in accord with your practical experience. Other studies show a trend towards the hardware becoming more reliable and the software becoming less reliable. This is chiefly because the software is becoming more complex and it is increasingly difficult to test millions of lines of code for all the likely situations where it is expected to operate. The other figures are reasonably consistent between the polls. The message is, even with data backup you have to take care to prevent data loss of new and changed working data between backups.

System Recovery

If your business relies on a network of computers to trade, it is important that any malfunction of the network is quickly rectified to prevent serious loss of income. A hardware malfunction is fixed by replacing hardware. Software and data (the image) loss is fixed by replacing the image: known as bare-metal recovery or HDD image recovery. You re-establish a computer network quickly by regularly backing-up *all* the images resident on the system, and, when the broken system is repaired, rewriting the stored backup image on to the system working media.

The above statement is deliberately general because of the great variety of computer network connections that can exist. A network may consist of two computers or many hundreds of computers, have one server or many servers, and so on with other characteristics. Software applications that provide complete system recovery have to take account of these differences, and as a result are more complex than backup software designed for business data only.

So system recovery software may be required to restore a single server image or a number of different server images; a single thin-client image, or a large number of identical thick-client images. The different servers have to be restored separately, but the identical clients can be restored semi-automatically. In other words, a working server can semi-automatically distribute a client operating system, together with the required applications, to every client workstation on the network, without loading it manually at each client workstation. This saves a deal of time when commissioning or recovering the network. The arrangement described above is common, but clearly, there are many other combinations possible, so you have to specify each system recovery method to meet your network needs.

If you have experienced a hard drive failure, you replace it, and you have a computer with blank hard drive: it has no operating system, so it cannot start by itself. For a restart, in most cases, you use a separate system recovery removable medium (widely known as a boot disk), inserted in the appropriate media drive and loaded (restart the computer). This medium holds an independent bootable operating system and software recovery tools which enable you to step though the system recovery process restoring the computer to operational status.

When your system is running normally, the system recovery software may also provide business data backup and restoration facilities in the same way as business data only backup software does. This can be a convenient way to specify business data and system recovery software.

System Recovery Testing

A typical system recovery software application requires that you save the complete hard disk drive image on to backup media. Then, in addition, you have to generate a system recovery removable medium for re-starting the computer that has failed (because it has no effective operating system). Typically, the system recovery removable medium is generated by the system recovery application and is unique to it.

To test the system recovery software application you need a computer with empty working media (or corrupted data which you can overwrite because it has no business value). The most direct method is to have one computer on the network with a second hard disk drive used exclusively for testing. Then, using the system recovery removable medium, you can restore the entire system from the backup media to the spare hard drive reserved for this purpose. To test the efficacy of the process you then have to restart (boot) from the recovered image and test that the transferred image works as expected. You will have to designate the spare hard drive as the working media for the duration of the test. Wipe the test hard drive clean before the next test, and bring the normal working hard drive back into service.

Guidance. *[The system recovery software application will guide you though the procedure for transferring the working media image to the backup medium. It will also guide you, using the system recovery removable medium instructions, in transferring the backup image on to the working media when required. The system recovery software application will overwrite everything on both the backup media (when backing up) and the working media (during restoration) when you carry out these procedures. Make sure there is no valuable data on the backup medium or the working medium which are used with the system recovery software.]*

There are other sorts of system recovery removable medium known as system rescue disks. They are bootable, carry an independent operating system and a number of general operating system recovery tools. These are not necessarily directly associated with the system recovery software. You can recover data from broken systems with them, and carry out fault-finding investigations to bring the computer back into normal operation. One problem with these rescue disks is that they require a high level of technical operating system knowledge to be used successfully. But if you have the expertise they can get you out of a lot of trouble.

Writing the Requirements Specification

Introduction

The whole point of a computer network is to connect together sources of business information that would otherwise be isolated to a few individuals. One constant staff complaint I have heard about business management is that "They never tell me what is going on, so I am kept in the dark like a mushroom". Organizing business information and allowing staff easy access to it will go a long way to rescuing them from the mushroom farm. It will also increase the effectiveness of your organisation. In addition, your company website can keep prospects informed about the products and services of your business. So that's why it's a worthwhile time investment specifying your information needs before thinking about the network characteristics. The requirements specification is the transition or bridge between the identification of business needs and the software and hardware making up the computer network.

Network Description

After defining your business information needs you will see the tasks to be carried out at each workstation. These tasks dictate the requirements of the computing equipment and software needed to complete the system. Typically, each workstation will run a computer operating system supporting the applications software needed for that position and, in addition, any local peripheral equipment needed to operate the workstation. Common peripheral equipment such as printers and scanners can be shared over the network. State where there is more than one user operating each workstation (because you'll need to arrange multi-user access). Produce a list to cover all the workstations. Include existing workstations, mobile workstations such as portable notebooks, tablet PCs, and hand-held personal digital assistants. Include future workstations that you may expect as the result of business expansion (simply mark them *future*). Describe outside organisations that you want to communicate with though external networks. Back inside, show where the workstations will be physically located within the business premises. Let the vendor join up all these points and you will have your network.

In the case of thin-clients, the applications will reside on the applications server. In the case of personal computer workstations, some of the applications will reside on the workstations and some on the server, depending upon the nature of the application.

The network operating system will be chosen by the vendor in response to your application software choices and other network requirements. If you already have standalone computers, then their operating systems may need to be changed to ensure they are network compatible.

Positioning Workstations

When considering the positioning of workstations, take into account the working environment of the business and the health and safety regulations of your jurisdiction. Label the workstations with a name or number for easy identification. Later on they will have logical (an electrical address on the network) identification as well. Make a sketch or drawing of the premises with the computer workstations marked out to add into the requirements specification. Show the electrical power points too, as additional points may be needed to power the workstations. Larger modern buildings have separate clean power outlets intended for information technology equipment. Use these for your computing equipment. Otherwise, you will need additional power conditioning equipment for your network system. The heading *'Power Supplies'* later gives more information on this subject. Do not place computer equipment hard against walls or office partitions where the cooling airflow would be restricted; or near to other heavy electrical office equipment such as laser copying machines, because they can cause electrical interference. Position the workstations to prevent direct daylight or interior lighting from reflecting off the screens.

Think where the wiring is to go. Up though the ceilings, down under the floors, around the skirting board, or in the building electrical wiring conduit. You may need some wireless links for awkward building layouts where it is impossible to run cables. At this stage do not show the actual network connections between workstations, because this will depend upon the physical network, which is not yet decided. The vendor will design the network and initially needs to know the distance between the workstations. Make provision for a server. This is the dedicated computer that is not normally used as a workstation, but runs the network instead. A server needs to go in a secure room with limited user access.

If you are using the building electrical conduit, there are two types in modern buildings: one type for mains power wiring and another for information technology wiring. If available, use the conduit intended for information technology equipment.

If there is only conduit for power and lighting it need not be a problem, but mention it on the requirement specification. The vendor may have to supply network wiring with additional screening to reduce interference from the existing power cabling.

Specifying Hardware

General Features

The commercial off-the-shelf computer, whether a server, personal computer or thin-client workstation, is a powerful machine that can run a wide range of software without difficulty. It is designed and manufactured in large numbers for a mass market made up of a diverse mix of users. Because the mass market is so large, the major vendors can take advantage of the economies of scale during manufacture, and keep the price down. To cater for the various needs of users, standard computing equipment is configurable, so that it can be set up to meet the needs of the different market sectors. Initially the equipment is set up to meet the needs of the largest market sector, such as businesses, home users and schools. This means set up or configured to run office applications such as word processing, spreadsheets, drawing programs, games, music, the Internet and email. Although you will need many of these applications on your workstations, the standard commercial configuration may not suit your needs for specialized software applications, such as computer aided design, or other scientific and engineering disciplines. Specify the network services (that is, the software application areas that you require) and the workstation physical attributes (such as disabled person access, specialized keyboards, voice inputs, rotatable displays, multiple displays, or very large displays) you require, before thinking about exactly what equipment you will need. The vendor, with guidance from you, will take care of the detail of choosing the equipment.

Workstation Computers

One feature that you need to consider early is whether or not you require the facility of the user loading software at each workstation. If you do not have this requirement, you can specify thin-client (diskless) workstations mentioned in *'Useful Network Knowledge'*, under the heading *'Diskless Workstations'*. The contents of the Requirements Specification will make the other features of the workstation computer obvious to the network designer; the ability to support the software and hardware specified, and the need to enhance the network performance to secure optimum network data throughput for instance.

There are some physical aspects to consider; such as whether you want the computer case flat on the desk, or in the form of an upright tower. Alternatively you may want it completely out of sight under the desk or elsewhere. If you are interested in aesthetics, there are slim versions of both horizontal and vertical cases that look good and save desk space. Some desktop models integrate the whole personal computer into a thin liquid crystal display monitor. This looks elegant at reception giving your business a high technology look.

Visual Display Units

Whether or not you have a comfortable computing experience will depend largely on the quality of the visual display unit (VDU) at your workstation. One with a poor visual performance will cause eye strain, headaches and other physical discomforts after only a few hours work. You should be able to interact with a VDU for a full working day without adverse affects on your work performance (but with short breaks). There are many visual performance metrics used in the development and testing of VDUs, but these are intended to be carried out by test engineers under controlled laboratory conditions: they are of little use to the user. So the way for a user to judge the performance of a VDU is to go and look at it operating, interact with it, and make subjective assessments about its visual performance. Clearly you need to limit the number of times that you do this; therefore you develop a short product list before setting out. Do this by reading manufacturer's literature and independent comparison reviews in computer magazines. If you already have stand-alone workstations in your business, you will be familiar with some types of VDUs and may be satisfied with these. In this case you might re-specify them. If not, arrange a trial viewing with a nearby computerised business or VDU supplier and see how you get on with various makes and types.

By and large you get what you pay for; but every so often an inexpensive VDU outperforms more expensive products and this knowledge can make a big difference to your financial outlay. The technology used is not as important as the visual performance. VDUs with high-end visual performance, for example, those for colour photography or colour printing, can cost as much as ten times the cost of a general purpose VDU. After the launch of new technology, the price of VDUs does go down with time as with other commercial off-the-shelf products, but not as rapidly, it seems, as other computing products. For this reason, and the relatively large financial outlay compared to other computer products, VDUs are kept for longer periods before upgrading.

Since the VDU that the vendors propose will be part of a network quotation you do not have complete control over what type of VDU is supplied. A knowledge of VDU visual performance will enable you to assess the suitability of the VDUs proposed; in addition, you have some control through the wording of the requirements specification. A VDU for general purpose professional office use would have a nineteen inch, flat, colour screen with a resolution of 1280x1024 pixels (dots) at a refresh rate of 60 Hz as a minimum requirement. The chapter *'Obtaining Your Spec-*

ified Needs' gives an example in the *'Requirements Specification'* of the additional wording required to characterise the visual performance.

Pointing Devices

A pointing device is a small hand-held object that controls the movement of the cursor on the screen of the computer visual display unit. The ubiquitous pointing device is the computer 'mouse'. It may be connected to the computer by a wire (cord), an electromagnetic transmission such as an infra-red or radio link. Most of the cordless types require batteries, and this can be a nuisance if they need replacing frequently. If you favour a cordless, specify the type which have rechargeable batteries and are parked in a recharging cradle when not in use. Since they all work perfectly well, look for one that you are comfortable with (a pleasant look and feel) as you will spend a lot of time interacting with this device.

Printers

The price of printers ranges from unbelievably cheap for the home user, to astonishingly expensive for commercial document production. A general-purpose office printer sits somewhere in the middle of the price range. A printer has a number of user characteristics that you have to specify for the vendor, these are:

- Paper size. The common international standard for general office use, such as business letters and forms is designated A4 (297 mm by 210 mm) by the International Standards Organisation (ISO). Another useful size is twice the size of A4 designated A3 (420 mm by 297 mm), which is useful size for engineering drawings, schematics and artwork. You will have to use a plotter to use larger paper sizes than these. Most printers can handle a range of metric and imperial paper sizes and envelopes by means of the physical adjustment of the input paper-tray mechanism, combined with a selection of parameters through the printer applications software. To change the paper size you have to change the paper in the input tray unless the printer has two or more input trays holding different paper sizes. Where you have multiple input trays you can switch between them though the printer applications software. The less expensive printers such as personal printers attached to a workstation rarely have multiple input trays because of the higher costs involved; but a shared network printer can be to a superior specification and include them for network user convenience.

- Paper weight. Typically general-purpose printers cater for a common range of paper weights such as 64 grams per square meter (g/m^2) to $188\,g/m^2$. Specify any non-standard requirements such as light paper, heavy paper or card, and transparencies outside of common weights.

- The duty cycle. This is expressed by stating the average number of pages that you expect to print each month from the printer. If you specify a printer with too low a duty cycle, it will soon become unreliable and a nuisance because of its frequent malfunction. In the longer term, the cost-of-ownership is reduced by purchasing a more expensive printer that exceeds your current requirements, but contributes to productivity because of its dependability.

- Print speed in pages per minute with a defined page image. This is usually text, expressed in a certain page coverage, such as eighty per cent. It does not mean that all pages will emerge in this time: the more complex the image the longer it takes. Anything below 20 pages per minute is frustratingly slow in my experience. Specify the speed for the common images that you print.

- Input and output paper tray capacities and number of trays. The heavy-duty cycle and faster printers have larger input and output tray capacities so that you are not reloading plain paper (and removing printed paper on larger print runs) too frequently. There should be enough input paper to last the working day so you do not have the distraction of reloading input paper during busy times. If you want to change paper sizes frequently, specify two or more input trays to hold the different paper sizes, different paper weights and different types of envelopes.

- Output image type. Describe the common type of image output that you generate, such as photographs, drawings, illustrations, printed word or all four mixed. This is because, for instance, printers designed for photographs will not give optimum performance producing the printed word. If you have mixed images specify a general-purpose office printer that is optimised for these; this will be suitable for your business.

- Resolution and image quality. For general-purpose office work the minimum resolution required is 600x600 dots per inch (dpi). If you want to print high quality photographic images, the resolution required may be much higher than this. Image quality is subjective. The image should not suffer from poor black and white definition, which means the text should be black, not grey, with letter edges sharp, not fuzzy; the shading should be smoothly graduated, and there should be no vertical or horizontal banding with solid images. With colour, all the above applies but you have the added requirement that the colours are reproduced accurately without tingeing. Tingeing is an overall bias towards one colour: the picture looks bluish or reddish for instance.

- You also need to know that the colours on the computer screen will not reproduce exactly (but they should be close) on the printer. This is because the process for producing colour is different on computer displays and printers; it is not a fault in the printer. If you require accurate print colour reproduction, you will need additional colour calibration software. This is often included in high-end graphical design applications. As with visual display units, read the independent reviews to acquire knowledge that is not mentioned in the marketing hyperbole, and then go and look at some demonstrations to make a final judgment against your specification.

- Double-sided printing. You can do double-sided printing on the less expensive printers by using the manual facilities provided by the printer applications software. It has the facility to print only even or odd numbered pages. So you print all the odd numbered pages first, select reverse print and even numbered pages, and then print all the even numbered pages backwards.

Guidance. [*To do this successfully there are two facts you need to know. One: Is the last page number odd or even? If the last printed page is numbered odd, then remove it from the paper stack, because the other side of it should be blank. If you fail to do this, the reverse print even page numbering will be incorrect and the print run will be ruined. Two: This is difficult to obtain; for any successful duplex print run there must be no paper mis-feeds. Therefore, you need to know the reliability of the printer paper-feed mechanism. If you ask the printer manufacturer the question "What is the failure-rate of the paper-feed mechanism," they will be reluctant to tell you. In practice, if you specify a failure rate to them, they will suggest a printer model that is likely, in their experience, to meet your specification. You express the paper-feed reliability in units of mis-picked paper sheets per total number of sheets. Miss-picking means the printer mechanism picks up more than one sheet at a time. It can also skew sheets which is counted as a failure too. So, if you print duplex documents hundreds of pages long, there must be no miss-feeds in hundreds of pages; thousands of pages long, no miss-feeds in thousands of pages, and so on. Specify your requirements in this way.*]

If your work requires frequent duplex printing, specify automatic double-sided printing (automatic duplex). This is available on most of mid-priced business printers, and always on those for commercial document production.

Scanners and Data Entry

Specify the practical scanning requirements you need. Here are the basics:

- Document type. Size, single sided or double sided, paper weight (thickness).

- Paper feed. Manual or automatic duplex.

- Image type. Black and white, grey-scale, or colour.

- Duty cycle. How many pages per month average.

- Resolution. 300 dpi upwards depending upon your needs. The more detail you need the higher the resolution required.

- Editing. Document clean-up, de-skew, de-speckle, text and image additions and corrections.

Guidance. [If you are converting from paper-based customer records to (for instance) electronic customer records on a database for the first time, then scanning the backlog of records into electronic form will require a high-speed scanner to get through the workload in reasonable time. In addition, well-used paper-based files showing signs of long use, in that they are curled, stapled, creased, stained and out of order, will need preparation before they can be scanned. This backlog scanning task is best allocated to a specialist in the document management field. Sorting out a well-used single paper customer file can take up to a quarter of an hour for each file. How many files do you have?]

For day-to-day electronic data entry into a database there are two considerations: entering the initial personal details of new customers, and updating existing electronic records during customer consultation. Staff can enter customer details though the keyboard as text and also scan in any diagrams, charts or images that may exist for that new customer. They may, during consultation, prefer to enter data in a number of different ways: keyboard and mouse, handwriting on an electronic tablet or by voice. Specify these different workstation data entry needs on the requirements specification.

The interfaces between the various methods of data entry and one or more records databases is an exercise in data management that the system designer will solve during the design process.

Servers

As we discussed before, a server is a central computer on the network that provides services to the user workstations distributed across the network. They are used for serving data files, running the applications software, providing local and wide area communications and hosting databases. They also act as backup machines for other servers on high reliability networks. A large network, geographically distributed supporting thousands of users, typically employs more than one server, each one carrying out a single specialized task. In a small to medium-size business, where a network would have tens to hundreds, rather than thousands of users, then its server would likely carry out a number of different concurrent tasks, rather than a single task; these are general-purpose servers. Servers work harder and for longer periods than do workstations; so they are designed to meet the additional workload. The list below describes features that indicate the suitability of a computer to act as a server:

- Convenient Hardware Maintenance. To service hardware you need to easily replace the interior sub-assemblies, so access to the inside of the computer is important. The sub-assembly wiring should go though electrical connectors (plugs and sockets) so that disconnection and reconnection is straightforward. The more expensive servers have 'hot swap' features: which means you can replace some sub-assemblies without removing power from the server; they slide in and out though the front panel.

- Convenient Software Maintenance. To service software you update it by loading the latest patches or software versions into the computer. You can do this easily either from removable media or from the Internet. All reputable vendors provide a service to do this.

- Straightforward Network Management. This enables the system administrator to easily set up and deploy network applications such as LAN messaging and collaboration services, shared external communication services, databases and user application programs. Network management software makes it easy to secure, troubleshoot, reconfigure the network and add or remove users.

- Expandable. As you become familiar with your computer network, you will develop new tasks for it that require more server file and applications space. As a result the server will need to expand its capacity for permanent and temporary memory storage (Hard Disk and Random Access memory). Also, it should have the facilities to connect to, and co-operate with, other new servers which you may need for future computing requirements.

- Speed. There are a number of technical factors that determine computer speed. The most obvious are the speed of the central processing unit (CPU) in gigahertz(GHz), and the amount of RAM fitted in gigabytes(GB). These characteristics, and the way the other parts of the computer are matched together determine the speed of the machine. From the user point of view, the server must be fast enough to support all the workstation users concurrently, so that each user will not experience frustration due to delays in the operation of their chosen application.

- Reliability. A server must be reliable because you depend on it so much, a lone server being a single point of failure on the network. A general approach to network reliability is described under the heading 'A Practical Approach to Reliability' in this chapter.

- Fault-tolerance. Fault-tolerance features increase the reliability of the server so that it remains in service without interruption. The provision of fault-tolerance relies on a particular combination of software and hardware architecture, so the software and the hardware together support the fault tolerance features of the server.

Software

General Characteristics

At this point I shall clarify what I mean by the general terms operating software, office productivity software, network security software and applications software. I mean software that is designed, developed, tested and deployed to an existing client base. That's software in proven use. Do not entertain the idea of ordering *custom designed* software for your business — the development risk is too great to shoulder for a typical small or medium-size business and high risk for large business. All the software that you will ever need for business is already written; take advantage of the completed product.

The vendor will need to *configure* your software: this is different from the software engineering process altogether and a *much* simpler than software development. Configuration consists of entering data, called parameters, into the established software to set it up to suit the particular system characteristics that you specify.

Office Productivity, Network Operating, and Network Security Software

If you want office productivity software to have special features, then use the technique described below under the heading *'Choosing Specialist Applications Software'*. Otherwise, note that the majority of office productivity software, such as word-processors, spreadsheets, databases, and drawing programs have been in existence for many decades, are mature products and most people have their favorites, perhaps from school-days. Often businesses have historical policies on this type of software so that everyone in the business can easily exchange information in a standard format. If this is the case, simply specify your preferences in the requirements specification. In contrast, network operating system and network security software are highly technical products so that here you specify only the objectives that you wish to achieve with the computing system, not name a particular application. There are examples of these objectives in the requirements specification.

Choosing Specialist Applications Software

Choosing the appropriate software in terms of user needs takes clarity of thought, effort and time; and is an essential early step of computer network implementation. It is one of the more complex activities of generating a requirements specification and consists of researching what is currently available, of learning the jargon and understanding the software capabilities. You cannot describe your business needs without *some* user knowledge of commercial-off-the-shelf software operation — you have to know what's possible. So, the process of generating business objectives in relation to software features and functions is an iterative process: you specify objectives, review available software, modify the objectives and so on.

If during this process you find software that you 'must have', because of its prize-winning features and widespread user acceptance, be cautious how you communicate this requirement to the system vendor. Do not purchase software directly from a software supplier, because then it can become unclear who is responsible for the integration of the software into the computer network. You may become the unfortunate victim of blame tick-tack, where each organisation passes off the blame for a problem to the other organisation — very frustrating for the end-user! Purchase the software through the system vendor, specifying that it is the vendor's responsibility to configure and integrate the software to meet your requirement specification.

An Example Derived from Business Needs

For an example we will take the operational area of sales order processing. The objectives of this area are to receive, process and dispatch customers orders in the shortest order fulfillment time to meet the customer's delivery expectations; and simultaneously reduce the bill payment cycle-time to improve business cash flow. Because it's software that the user sees and interacts with, the objectives are expressed mainly in terms of software characteristics. Software to achieve these objectives has to provide an administrative resource to generate a profile of each customer, track each customer from order entry to product or service delivery, bill the customer, and submit the payment to the accounts section for recording, all in a specified time. Moving on to some measurable characteristics we can develop a list by which you can judge the software's ability to meet your needs. The list below shows examples of (simplified) sales order processing software characteristics. The first two items are general for all software in a small business.

Sales Order Processing (Example)

Introduction

The software shall provide an effective semi-automated means of entering, recording and delivering the goods or services described in our customer's purchase orders. It shall enable our business to deal with purchasing issues such as multiple order sources, order changes, partial shipments, back orders, stock control, different payment methods and invoicing. When required, our customers shall be informed of the main order processes such as delivery date, order awaiting stock, shipment date and payment arrangements.

Input Screens General Characteristics

The user screen interfaces shall be Graphical User Interfaces (GUIs) consisting of pictures, icons, buttons and dialogue boxes. Each screen shall be user configurable so that the visible concurrent images can be selected by the user. The interfaces shall be intuitive to an extent that allows a newcomer to the application, after four hours training from an experienced user, to operate the basic features of the application. In addition the application shall provide context-sensitive help functions that enable newcomers, after an initial period of training and use, to further train themselves to use the additional functions of the software. The same help material shall be supplied as a user manual. Where required, the supplier shall provide instructor-led training on the use of the basic features of the application. Amongst the standard functions provided by the application, the input screens shall provide the functions listed below:

- The layout of the screen shall be logical to the user (Ask the user).

- Navigation to related screens shall be selected with a single click of the pointing device. Keyboard key combinations shall also be available.

- Errors in data entry shall be corrected without difficulty (Undo functions).

- Input data that requires validation shall be entered though dialogue boxes providing input masks and associated error messages to guide the user into adopting the correct input format.

- Input screens shall have access to a 'training sandbox' where the users can practice and learn the skills required to operate the application without disrupting the normal operation of the application.

Order Entry

The order entry screens shall provide the functions described below:

- At the business's Internet site, provide semi-automated input screens so that customers can place their order. They shall be able to specify the product details, preferences and associated details of price, tax, delivery time, customer's address, shipping address, email address, credit card details or other agreed method of payment details. The customer shall not be charged until the goods are shipped. The customer shall be able to communicate directly with Sales to change order details or obtain clarification on the product characteristics.

- For non-Internet orders, enter the customer's order with the associated details of price, tax, delivery time, customer's address, shipping address, email address, credit card details or other agreed method of payment details. The customer shall not be charged until the goods are shipped.

- Deal with customer order changes, cancellations and refunds, partial shipments, back orders, and method of shipment.

- Provide facilities to generate a new customer template to be set up by customers (via Internet) or in-house staff to facilitate rapid data entry for future orders.

- Integrate with various national and international credit card authorization schemes.

- Show stock levels and automatically update the current stock levels and customer account balances.

Stock Control

The stock control screen shall provide the functions described below:

- Provide multi-location stock control.

- Support Last In First Out (LIFO) and First In First Out (FIFO) stock handling.

- Allow multiple suppliers for each item.

- Allow multiple price levels and price breaks.

- Track, re-order point, and stock levels per item.

- Track best/last cost, economic order quantities and lead time per item.

- Display inventory templates for stock item additions.

Billing

The billing screen shall provide the functions described below:

- Facilitate recurring and incidental billing.

- Allow multiple billing periods to bill as often as needed.

- Provide multiple billing terms such as weekly, bi-monthly, quarterly and annually.

- Provide customer statement reprint for any prior billing period.

- Support emailing customer bills in HTML.

- Allow template customization of electronic HTML bills.

- Schedule user reports at set times or intervals to print or email.

Shipping

The shipping screen shall provide the functions described below:

- Generate picking lists for production to make up customer's order.

- Format and print packing slips and address labels.

- Provide a Freight Estimator for quotations.

- Generate a shipping manifest which interfaces with common freight carriers.

- Record package tracking numbers from freight carriers.

- Provide email notification of shipment to customers with Internet access for customer tracking of package.

Guidance. *[The above list is a guide and therefore not complete — it's to show you the process involved. Software of this type can have three to four hundred functions supporting its features: you have to know what you need for your business before you are faced with the full number available. Facing so many functions at once can be confusing if you are not prepared. As described earlier in this chapter, to develop your complete list, meet with your people who carry out this type of work, and ask them to describe additional functions that are important to them in their everyday work. Add these to the list to complete it. All these characteristics are written into the requirements specification under the appropriate software heading, along with the other network specifications. Therefore your software needs are transmitted to the vendors by means of the requirements specification document.]*

Defining Data Backup and System Recovery

For deciding which data to back-up and how often to back up, see under the heading *'Which Data'* and *'How Often'* in the chapter *'Useful Network Knowledge'*.

Backup Medium Capacity

To work out the quantity of data (in megabytes/gigabytes) to save during a day's single *full* data backup, we will use the widespread client-server model. Identify the largest file types that are likely to be used in your business. For guidance, Table 1, File Size Ranges, in the section *'Network Performance'* in chapter *'Useful Network Knowledge'* shows the expected file sizes against file types. If you are making estimates, the file size depends upon the file type. Text files are the smaller, with graphic, sound and video being much larger in ascending order. A file with a combination of text and graphics can be one thousand times the size of a text-only file. The daily minimum (full) business data backup media capacity is:

daily business data generated at each workstation × number of workstations.
For example 200 MB × 6 = 1200 MB per day.

Note that the data will be consolidated on the server HDD file-system and transferred (backed-up) to the backup medium elsewhere.

If you want to employ *unattended* backup, the capacity of a single removable medium must be large enough to save all the daily data files that require backing up at the time. If it isn't possible, because the capacity of a single piece of medium is not large enough to accommodate all the data files, then the only solution is to employ an automatic media changer. Ideally, apart from routine servicing, this has to be reliable enough to operate unattended for the duration of the system life.

Backup Time

Specify how long you want daily (full) business data backup to take; considering that the shorter the specified backup time the greater the expense of backup equipment. If you have chosen to back-up after normal office hours you will have plenty of time available, so that you can back-up unattended over several hours (if need be). The restoration time will be of a similar order but somewhat longer, because the systems administrator has to manually handle the business data media set.

The vendor will work out (or know from experience) the average business data transfer (backup) speed and offer suitable backup software and equipment to meet your criteria.

$$\text{Business data backup time} = \frac{daily\,business\,data\,backup\,size\,(MB)}{average\,business\,data\,transfer\,speed\,(MB/sec)}\ sec$$

Note that the *system* backup and restoration time (see *'System Recovery'* below), will be considerably longer than the business data backup time, because the system image is so much larger than the business data image alone. The calculation is similar, replace *'daily business data'* with *'whole HDD image'* and *'business data transfer'* with *'whole HDD image transfer'*.

Backup Software

Specify the features below; most professional backup software will have these. If there are a few missing from the vendor's proposal, then you can decide whether you can do without them or not at the time. The backup software in combination with the backup hardware shall provide the features listed below:

- Network operation by backing up files which are local or distributed across a computer network.

- A a graphical user interface so that the backup operation is possible by a trained but non-technical person.

- On-line help.

- Data compression to reduce the size of backup files.

- User file selection for backup, restoration and file exclusion.

- Full, incremental or differential backup.

- Scheduling of unattended backups.

- User selectable data transfer verification, error correction and reporting.

- Preservation of dated revisions by user selection; overwriting, appending and archiving files.

- User selectable encryption for nominated backup files.

- Data shredding for the elimination of selected files (to conform to privacy laws).

- Management of a variety of backup equipment(hardware) to allow for future changes in backup methods.

The above will cover the requirements which are common in a typical business.

System Recovery

System recovery software differs from data recovery software in that it is not *selective* in its recovery process. It copies the *whole image* of the system in permanent memory (HDD) and writes it elsewhere. The idea is, if you lose your operating system together with its applications and data, you can restore the whole system from a backup image to the working permanent memory (HDD). You will then have a working system without separately reinstalling the system, applications software and business data, which is a time consuming process. The complexity of the process is hidden from the user by the software user interface. This provides a simple procedure of invoking system recovery when the occasion demands it.

But notice, that to obtain an up-to-date hard drive image, you must have recently backed-up a copy, otherwise you will have lost the business data generated between the last backup and the current lost image. To overcome this problem, system recovery software typically separates the system image and the data image, so that you can specify an acceptable frequency of data backup independent of system backup. Alternatively you can use two separate backup applications, one for system and one for business data, these are sometimes incorporated into one suite of backup software.

System recovery applications software varies in its complexity from simple for a small number of computers (say tens) to complex for a large number of computers (say hundreds). Reduce the complexity of the problem by stating what your backup requirements are in plain English. Some of the basic features of system backup are shown below:

- Provide centralized management of system recovery and business data backup of all network computers.

- Have the ability to backup and recover databases.

- Be able to deploy a complete workstation recovery image to any network workstation.

- Have the capability to deploy a complete recovery image to workstation hardware that is of a *different* configuration to that from which the system data was first obtained (adaptable recovery). This is often called adaptable cloning or replicating systems.

- Provide labeling and catalogue of backup information and data for archiving and future restoration or recovery (historical system snapshots).

Backup Equipment

There are two types of backup equipment: internal and external. The internal fits inside the server or workstation in an equipment bay designed for the purpose, and the external is a separate piece of equipment connected to the network. Your backup requirements, the network configuration and the price, determine which type you need. In some sectors of industry the specifications for the backup process may well be determined by the regulatory demands imposed upon business computerisation — check with the authorities.

Total Permanent Memory (HDD) Size

Estimate all the business data files that you need to store over a specified period of time on the server hard drive. Add an amount for the operating system and applications, and include a generous allowance for future expansion. If you are planning a database of customer records, contact the software vendor to ascertain the database file sizes when the database is *populated* with your customer data. A database may be a separate application, or it may be embedded into a business application such as Sales Order Processing. So the formula for estimating the total permanent memory size (HDD) goes like this:

daily data generated at each workstation × number of workstations × number of working days.
For example 200 MB/day × 6 workstations × 220 days = 264,000 MBs.

Add 20 GB for the operating system and applicatons, giving the total of 284 GB. The next larger HDD size with a generous allowance for expansion is, say, 500 GB.

Power Supplies

Main Electricity Supplies

It's tempting to assume that everyone in your country knows about the characteristics of the main electricity supply, so you don't have to mention it in the requirements specification. Do mention it. If you don't specify what you require, then it becomes difficult to rectify mistakes made by a careless vendor or a distant supplier in the equipment supply chain. For one reason or another, vendors do occasionally supply computing equipment set to the wrong supply voltage. In most cases, when discovered, it is easily rectified by changing wiring links or switches inside the equipment. Providing, of course, that you haven't already connected low voltage equipment to a higher voltage mains supply and switched on. The result of which can be both spectacular and dangerous.

The nominal mains supply voltages are 115 Volts Alternating Current (VAC) at a frequency of 50 or 60 Cycles Per Second (CPS) (alternatively the unit Hertz may be used, which means the same thing but in metric units) or 230VAC also at a frequency of 50CPS or 60CPS. There are variations on these nominal values depending upon the region, district or country in which you reside. If you are in a remote area, contact the state or national electricity utility of your region to obtain the supply characteristics and availability of the supply in case they are different from the norm.

Most computing equipment will handle the expected voltage and frequency variations around the nominal without difficulty. For example common input voltage ranges are 85VAC to 135VAC; and 170VAC to 270VAC; and a common input frequency range is 48CPS to 62CPS. Some of the more sophisticated equipment has an extended input voltage range, covering all the common mains supply voltages. Through its electronics, it selects the correct voltage input range automatically.

Electricity supply utilities have a public service contract managed in conjunction with a government regulating authority concerned with the integrity of the public energy supply. This contract specifies the level of service provided to the public in terms of voltage, frequency, purity of waveform and continuity of service. Electricity supply utilities give an undertaking to supply energy to the stated specification for finite lengths of time. They do not claim to provide a continuous supply of energy; but you have to contact them to obtain the details of their service commitment. In industrialised countries they do well enough, so that most people consider that for practical purposes the electricity supply to be continuous. But if you are operating computer equipment and wish to protect your data then you have to know that the electricity supply is subject to perturbations that can corrupt or destroy computer data. Therefore, to counter this, you need to take steps to protect the integrity of the data stored in your computing equipment.

To give you some idea of the imperfection of the mains electricity supply, here is a list of the well understood perturbations:

- Blackout. This means total failure of the utility power — it turns off. It is caused by excessive demand by consumers, lighting strikes and other natural disasters, ice on exposed power lines, motor vehicle accidents, building earthworks, and even terrorist sabotage. If your computing equipment does not disconnect itself from the mains supply automatically, then switch it off manually because the mains supply restoration can be intermittent and contain the potentially damaging perturbations described below.

- Sag. This is a short-term reduction in the supply voltage. It is caused by increased local demand on the supply, such as that caused by the nearby start-up of heavy electrical machinery, especially when many people start up machinery at the same time such as on an industrial estate in the morning. In addition the power utility can lower the supply voltage for longer periods (hours to days) as a matter of operational policy. This is to maintain supply in periods of unusual peak demand. They rarely advise you of this action at the time, unless you have set up an operations communication agreement with them beforehand. Some electricity supply utilities make this information available on the Internet. Sags limit the power needed to run computing equipment reliably if the supply voltage falls outside the equipment's specification. This can result in malfunctions such as frozen software and system crashes leading to corrupted data.

- Spike. A spike is a narrow, almost instantaneous (millionths of a second), large increase (tens, hundreds or thousands of times the norm) in the supply voltage. It is commonly the result of a nearby lighting strike but is also generated by switching heavy electrical machinery on and off. Spikes can enter computing equipment directly though electrical wires (conductors) such as the mains supply connection or through less obvious wiring paths such as data networks and telecommunication connections. They can also enter indirectly through electrical induction (see below). Spikes can lead to equipment damage and corrupted data.

- Surge. A surge is a short (hundredths of a second) increase (tens) in the supply voltage. It is typically caused by switching off heavy electrical equipment such as air conditioning and building lifts or escalators. Surges can lead to equipment damage if the increase in supply voltage exceeds the equipment's input surge supply voltage specification by a large margin.

- Electrical Noise. The technical terms for electrical noise are Electo-Magnetic Interference (EMI) or Radio Frequency Interference (RFI). Computing equipment is protected against obvious sources of electrical noise interference such as fluorescent lighting, radio, television and mobile phone transmissions, but electrical noise is also generated by the perturbations mentioned above in varying degrees of intensity.

These power supply perturbations damage equipment in the following ways. If the disturbance is a fast electrical waveform such as from spikes and EMI, then although the electrical energy contained in them is low (except for nearby lightning strikes), they enter the computing equipment by electrical induction. There does not need to be a direct wiring connection between the source of the disturbance and the computing equipment or its sub-assemblies. The damage done by electrical induction usually takes the form of data loss or corruption rather than equipment failure. If the disturbance is a surge, then it arrives direct though the mains supply wiring. It is possible for a surge containing enough energy, to permanently damage equipment though overheating or breaking down electrical insulation. The equipment will need repair. A sag will cause equipment malfunction during the time that it is occurring, but the equipment will most likely function normally again when the supply voltage is restored.

The information provided below is to give you an idea of what you will need in a typical computer system. Bear in mind that you only need complete protection for equipment containing data. You do not need protection for the more robust equipment such as printers and displays for instance. Although lighting protection may be a sound investment for all equipment. Figure 7, LAN Power Supply Protection, shows the protection likely to be needed for a typical computer network.

Un-interruptible Power Supply

The most common method of protecting a computer is by means of an uninterruptible power supply (UPS). This power supply has the primary task of detecting an interruption of the mains supply and providing an alternative electricity supply for a *limited* time to allow the computer to shut down in an orderly manner. This prevents loss or corruption of computer data. The secondary task of an un-interruptible power supply is to filter or condition the mains supply to attenuate any electrical disturbances on it. This ensures that the supplied power is clean so as not damage the computer or its data. If the UPS does not have a line conditioner incorporated, then you will need a separate one installed near the computer equipment power outlet upstream of the UPS (unless you have clean IT mains supply outlets as part of the building power supply facilities).

The UPS operates for a limited time only because its alternative electricity supply is derived (after transformation) from an internal battery. Once the battery is exhausted the UPS switches off. By this time the computing equipment must have completed its shut-down. To ensure that the computer has completed its shut-down before the UPS switches off, the UPS and the computing equipment have to be matched. This consists of adding the total power requirement of the computing

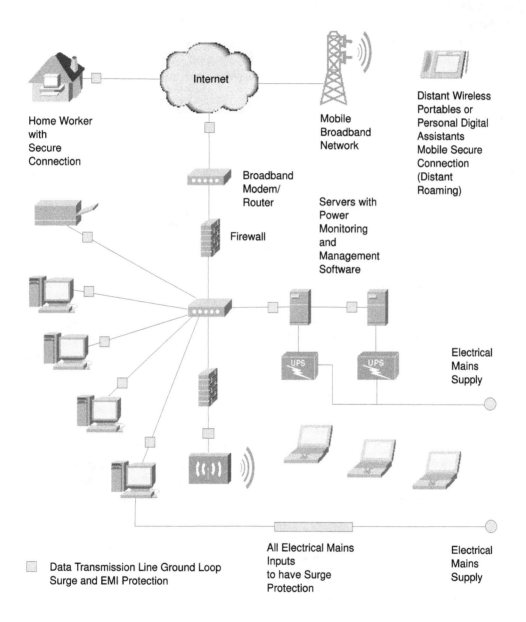

Figure 7: LAN Power Supply Protection

equipment and choosing an UPS which can supply the required power over the period of the shut-down cycle. There should be a safety factor of twenty five per cent added to the time to allow for variations in the shut-down cycle. Since in the early stages of project the computing equipment power consumption will not be accurately known, you will have to leave this calculation to the vendors. To witness the soundness of their calculations, request that during commissioning they carry out the test of pulling the mains supply plug on the server and other working computers, and checking that it shuts down safely and restarts in working order.

Emergency Power Supply

If you want to run your computer network independently from the electrical mains then you need an emergency power supply. This provides power from an independent generator such as one driven by a diesel engine, windmill or solar collector (with their associated power storage systems). This type of equipment takes time to start up; producing transient disturbances even with automatic changeover, so you will still need an UPS and line conditioner to protect your computing equipment.

Earthing or Grounding

Mains line conditioners and un-interruptible power supplies rely on the integrity of the mains supply neutral and earthing wiring systems in the building for their correct operation. This means that the neutral and earth connections must be wired according to the national electricity supply regulations. Because this is law, you may be tempted to assume that all building wiring systems are in good order and suitable for the operation of sensitive electronic equipment. This may not be the case. Engage the services of the national electricity supply organisation or their agents to test the integrity and safety of the building electricity supply to see that it is suitable for sensitive electronic equipment. The earth or grounding wiring must be of low impedance to the earth so that the wiring is free of electrical noise. In some older buildings you may require the wiring to be modified to meet updated modern regulations. The vendors who supply line conditioners and UPS equipment give extensive advice on this subject and may have a licensed representative in the area willing to survey your building.

Clean Power Supply

Modern business premises frequently have a dedicated mains power supply intended solely for information technology equipment. This is a clean stabilised mains supply taken to standard wall outlets which are labelled or colour tagged for easy identification. It derives its input from the standard mains supply, so it fails when the mains fail, unless there is an emergency power supply provided as well. So yes, you do still need an UPS but not a line conditioner.

A Practical Approach to Reliability

Because of a lack of reliability-engineering expertise in a typical business, you adopt a practical approach to network reliability. Look at the experience of others in a comparable situation; talk to other businesses in your area, and also research other independent sources on network reliability as follows:

- Surveys carried out and published by trade associations and chambers of commerce. These surveys provide reliability figures derived from formal studies on a number of established business computer networks. Typically these surveys are free or low cost to organisation members.

- Surveys carried out and published by independent laboratories associated with major computer magazine publishers. These are also free or low cost to magazine subscribers.

- Surveys carried out and published by independent consultants for sale to the computer industry. These are likely to be the more expensive but also the most extensive.

Some general guidelines of obtaining a reliable network are:

- Seek out the available surveys as described above. These will indicate whose equipment or software is the more reliable.

- Choose vendors with a good reputation. The business computing group of your business association, government small business help organisation, or your professional learned institution, will most likely have a reliable vendors list. This is a good starting point.

- Ask for system components that are branded: that is, possess a company name or trade mark. Although many standard computer parts are manufactured in the same factory, the branded parts have more stringent quality controls placed upon them during manufacture, and are therefore more reliable.

- These days, servicing of computer equipment is by sub-assembly replacement, because this is the economic way to repair. In turn, the sub-assemblies, because of the intricate way they are manufactured, are not often repairable and are thrown away. So the practical way to keep your network operative is to employ branded equipment and software with a good reputation; and then run diagnostic software at regular intervals to detect poor equipment and network performance, which often precedes network failure. If the network does break down, the diagnostic software used by your system administrator or vendor's service technician will find faults to sub-assembly level where the sub-assemblies can be quickly replaced.

Availability Figure Percentage	Network Downtime in Hours per Year	Typical of Service Type
99.00% (two nines)	87.60 hours (3.65 days)	Internet Service
99.90% (three nines)	8.76 hours	Small Business Server
99.99% (four nines)	0.876 hours (52 mins)	Enterprise Server
99.999% (five nines)	0.0876 hours (5.2 mins)	Telecommunications
99.9999% (six nines)	0.00876 hours (0.52 mins)	A Target to Aim For!

Table 4: Network Failure Times

To give you some idea about reliability and availability, Table 4, Network Failure Times, shows percentage availability against the time the network is *in*operative per year (assuming the network is running 8760 hours annually).

Specify the availability of a network in business terms, for example, apart from scheduled maintenance; 'the network shall not fail more than once a year and restoration time shall not exceed four hours'.

Connections to Outside Networks

To make full use of your LAN you will need to access the numerous information services available on the Internet provided by many organisation's wide area networks (WANs). The interface between your LAN, the Internet and outside WANs is mature, and your vendor will be able to deploy such an interface using commercial off-the-shelf equipment and software. Government organisations, the civil service and large commercial organisations such as private insurance funds may have their own interface specifications standards and guides that cover every aspect of the connection. These specifications are intended, primarily, for business software developers to ensure that the developer's software can interface with the organisation's WAN. Your involvement will be to ensure that the business software that you intend to adopt meets the interface requirements of the organisations that you need to deal with; in addition to that, you specify who has workstation access to universal or specialised information services. There is an example in the requirements specification.

Network User Access

A network user can log-on to the LAN with their user-name and password but not have access to all the resources and data provided by the network. This is because the network operating system (NOS) provides a utility to afford or deny user access to the various resources such as software applications, directories, files, printers, other computers, and WANS. This utility is part of the network management software and it appears under a variety of names such as User Access Control, Password Properties, User Manager, Trustee Rights and others depending upon whose network operating system you are using. The method of assigning user access rights is different in detail only, for each type of network operating system.

To enable you to manage the network in an organised and secure manner, the ability to grant and withdraw user access rights is confined to one person, normally the network system administrator. No-one else, because it is easy to cause confusion due to lack of rigor in granting access, and thereby compromising the security of your network.

User access rights or permissions as they are called, are able to be selected for *each user* where, for instance, technical aspects of the network are accessible only to a technical qualified person, but access to customers records would be denied to that person, and available to only to marketing people. To avoid the complication of assigning individual rights to every new user, network operating systems provide methods of assigning users to groups. Each group has pre-defined access rights, say to a number of software applications, directories, files, workstations, printers and the Internet; adding a new user to this group gives them access to the group's resources. Some NOSs arrange groups in a hierarchy where the top group inherits the privileges of lower groups; this feature is most useful in larger networks with many users.

In addition to managing user network access, there is an additional task which is to manage the technical parameters and configuration of the network. This is something that is necessary when the network is first set up and tested; when the network is changed to accommodate new users; and sometimes after restoring the network to service after a malfunction. If your network administrator has the technical skills they can take care of these tasks; otherwise the vendor's service technicians who are contracted to maintain your system should do it.

Although users may have restrictions placed upon them as to the resources and data they may access on the network, they are not restricted from making *user* preferences at their workstation. User preferences give the user the ability to control the look and feel of their software interface. This feature is provided by all network operating systems and also by all applications programs.

User File Access Permissions

User file access is an extension or additional layer of security to protect file content from unauthorized access. It enables the system administrator to decide which users have access rights or permissions to particular files on the network. The system administrator has *administration* rights over all files, in effect, *ownership* of all files on the system. He/she has the ability to create user groups, change file permissions, create, delete, read and write files without restriction. The system administrator grants two types of file access to users. These are *full access* and *partial access*. Full access enables the user to create and delete content, and to read and write files; it's for those users who are involved in document creation. Users who are granted full access to particular files can choose to share those files with others or not. They have *user ownership*. Partial access restricts users to read-only, for those users who are after information only, and are not involved in the creation process. They do not enjoy file ownership.

Define the user access rights by drawing up a table and insert this into the requirements specification. Table 5, User Permissions, shows the general approach (one table for each user).

Documentation

Documentation promotes understanding between you and the vendor, and it also keeps the lines of communication open between members of your project team. Documentation enables you to track the progress of the project, control changes in your requirements and gather contributions from project members. It clarifies verbal communication, reduces confusion in everyone's mind, and so increases the chances of project success. There are three main areas of documentation:

- One is concerned with the internal communication between project members.

- Two is concerned with defining the project objectives between the business and the vendor.

- Three is concerned with the user configuration, operation and maintenance of the completed network supplied by the vendor.

The first area of documentation is described in the chapter *'Management Issues and How To Get Started'* and the second in this chapter *'Writing the Requirements Specification'*. The third area of documentation is the subject of this section *'Documentation'*.

Network Documentation

The documentation supplied with network computing equipment by the vendor will determine how easily you can operate the network during its working life. Good documentation reduces the cost of ownership. From experience, I know that documentation is rarely a priority with engineers, so it tends to be relegated (for attention) to the end of the design project. Here, too often, it is completed poorly in a rush. This is a disadvantage to the end–user. You can discourage this type

Individual User Permissions or Group Permissions: Y=Yes, N=No; Usr1=Create, Delete, Read/Write; Usr2=Read Only.

User Permissions and Network Resource Allocated	Reception	Administration	Sales	Purchasing	Stores	Engineering
User name issued	Y	Y	Y	Y	Y	Y
User password issued	Y	Y	Y	Y	Y	Y
Local printer	Y	Y	Y	Y	Y	Y
Shared printer	Y	Y	Y	Y	Y	Y
Customer records	Y, User2	N	Y, User1	Y, User2	N	N
Office Administration Files	Y, User2	Y, User1	N	N	N	N
Financial Files	N	Y, User1	N	N	N	N
Network configuration(System Administrator only)	N	N	N	N	N	
Internet	N, User2	Y, User2	Y, User2	Y, User2	Y, User2	Y, User2
WAN 1	Y, User2	Y, User2	Y, User2	Y, User2	Y, User2	Y, User2
And so on....						

Table 5: User Permissions

89

behaviour by stating what you want in the way of documentation in the requirement specification. This causes the vendor to think about documentation early in the project, and to include a realistic amount of time and expertise for its creation.

The vendor designs the network largely from standard manufactured parts and software. The manufacturers and software providers send documentation with their products, so that the vendor can understand and properly use them. These documents are predominantly technical in nature and are intended for network engineers, so are of little use to network end–users (except for the software applications user manuals which the vendor will pass on to you). Sometimes, especially on smaller projects, the vendor supplies manufacturer's documentation in lieu of useful network end–user documentation. To ensure the vendor supplies user documentation that is of practical value, you specify the contents in advance. First though, you must tell the vendor what the level of understanding the members of the business have after they have undergone training. This is so that the vendor can set the technical level of the user manual. Here is a guide to the contents of a useful network-operating manual:

- Vendor information, contact and location details, document authorisation (sign-off) and arrangements for future updating and version control (if any).

- A vendor statement that the supplied network system conforms to the product liability, health and safety, customer privacy and data security legislation for the jurisdiction in which you operate. This statement shall appear in the manual front matter.

- User CAUTIONS or WARNINGS which apply to the system. These shall appear in the manual front matter.

- A general description of the 'as installed' network; its topology, its equipment and installed software (including software version numbers). The network connection cables numbering system.

- A description on how to operate the network. How to safely start, log-on, log-off and shut down the network. There shall be examples of normal network behaviour by means of screen shots, diagrams and symbols. An explanation of user access rights. How to use the data backup features and how to recover the network after a system crash.

- A technical description in simple language, but of sufficient technical depth to enable a systems administrator (independent of the vendor) to reconfigure the network after making changes or extending the network to accommodate new user requirements.

- The detailed configuration settings of each workstation, server and associated computing equipment. Each configuration shall include (where applicable):

the administrative name of the product and serial number; the physical network address; the logical network address and the type of network interface card. Other information as required to maintain the equipment such as internal switch positions and links.

- A description of the steps that the user can take to maintain the network in good order.

- A list of suppliers associated user manuals required to operate the network applications software and network hardware.

- An explanation of the initial user rights and licensing arrangements for the installed software.

- A description of the warranties offered by the vendor and its suppliers.

Include a documentation supply schedule with reviews in your project plan. This is so that you can decide early on in the project if the manual style and contents meet your needs, the vendor needs time to change them if you are dissatisfied. A good starting point to understanding what the vendor is likely to supply is to look at the previous manuals that the vendor has supplied to past customers. You can use the above contents guide to make an assessment.

Conformance to Regulatory Standards

Regulatory standards are derived from government legislation. Conformance to regulatory standards, international, national and local, are an effective way of dealing with the legal framework that applies to a business network. Conforming to equipment safety standards, and the prevention of electrical interference standards are the responsibility of the equipment and network designers. Conforming to customer privacy, data security and health and safety at work standards are the responsibility of the network operator. Where there are no applicable standards, look for established codes of good practice which guide you in the ethical use of your network.

Equipment Standards

The manufacturers of commercial-off-the-shelf computer equipment have to sell large numbers into sophisticated global markets, so their products are tested and certified by the recognised equipment certification agencies of each major market. The common certifications are for user safety, meeting the Health and Safety Regulations, and electromagnetic interference (EMI), meeting the Electromagnetic Compatibility Regulations. Certified equipment is safe to use and will not cause interference to, or suffer interference from, other electrical equipment. These certifications are valid provided that the equipment is used according to the manufacturer's instructions, is not physically damaged, is correctly installed (there are standards for cabling) and has not been modified (except to the permitted manufacturer's instructions for the purpose of system configuration).

A reputable vendor will factory-test your equipment, deliver it and site-test it as a system at your business, so that you will see everything is in good order. If you are taking delivery of equipment only, inspect it for physical damage, then follow the instructions in the user's operating manual. Send damaged equipment back to the vendor without meddling with it.

Customer Privacy and Data Security

This is another view of network security and backup from the point of view of interested international, national and state regulators. These official organisations have an interest, considering the common good of society, in how you go about handling business information in your organisation. Their laws and regulations about customer privacy which apply to paper records, also apply to electronic information stored on, or transmitted across, a computer network, hence data security. Because official organisations are concerned with all business information they call it Information Security rather than data security, but for the purpose of explanation here, the terms are interchangeable. Regulations about customer privacy restrict the type of people to whom you knowingly give customer information, and also apply to the way that you meet statutory and regulatory demands of security, confidentiality, and civil evidence. So they are regulations about your business behaviour. Each jurisdiction has customer privacy laws and regulations, and, in addition, these will vary by business or industrial sector. If you are already in business you will, most likely, know the regulations which apply to you; if not, a useful place to acquire information is with your local business association.

So customer privacy implies data security, which means preventing unauthorised access to customer details and other data. The international standards which lay down the established rules for customer privacy and data security are *'ISO 27001 Model for establishing, implementing, operating, monitoring, reviewing, maintaining, and improving an Information Security Management System'*. There are useful *guidelines* in the related security code of practice *'ISO 27002 Established guidelines and general principles for initiating, implementing, maintaining, and improving information security management within an organisation'*. Note that ISO 27002 contains the guidelines which help you understand and apply ISO 27001 to your business. Both are complex documents, so I have listed the basics below to get you started:

- Formulate a business policy on customer privacy and data security.

- Invoke access restrictions. Logging on by proof of user identification and alpha–numeric password codes, or physical characteristics such as fingerprint or iris identification.

- Differentiate between levels of access to various parts of the network by logged-on users. Some users will be allowed read-only, others will be allowed to read and write, and a restricted number change the network configuration and carry out backup and maintenance.

- Provide of an electronic audit trail. Employ software that identifies and records the actions of each user logged on to the network. The audit record should be saved during the routine backup procedure.

- Encrypt files that are transmitted outside the business.

- Automate log-off after a defined period of user inactivity.

- Shred (destructively erase) discarded data. When a computer holding customer information reaches the end of its life, its permanent (hard disk) data must be destructively erased. The normal file erase feature of servers and workstations does not immediately erase the data: it only makes it inaccessible to the system, so that the erased file space can be overwritten later by new data. This makes the erased data recoverable to someone with expert knowledge and the appropriate software. You need data shredding software to permanently erase customer or other sensitive data on a computer destined for disposal.

- Install network security software to provide protection from malicious intrusion from external networks such as the Internet.

Information Security Compliance.

The starting point is to state the information security standard you need in the requirements specification. Many vendors have pre-designed (but flexible) systems which meet existing information security standards in your business or industrial sector. When the computer system is installed and operational it is designed to meet your chosen information security standard. If you need to reassure you customers that you know what you are doing, then, in addition, you will need to get your computer system audited and certified against the chosen standard. This is done by an independent certification body. The certification body may be called a registration body or registrar depending on the jurisdiction in which they operate. If you are successful at passing the audit the certification body will give you a "Certificate of Conformity", which you proudly display on your letterhead and web site. To keep your system certified it will need auditing at regular intervals, typically once a year.

The decision to obtain information security compliance is a business strategic one. In many businesses you will be obliged to ensure that your computer system is compliant to existing information technology laws and regulations. Whether, or not, you choose to meet the particular standard mentioned above, or a sector specific standard depends upon the type of business you are in. The process followed to meet the requirements of certification varies somewhat between countries and sometimes between states within countries, but most industrialised countries have a unified national system based on the international standard.

Installation and Test

One of the most useful contributions you can make towards installation and test is to write a clear requirements specification and project schedule. Installation and test by its nature is disruptive to normal business operation; so the better the vendor understands your needs, the shorter the period of disruption. It is customary to schedule this activity at weekends, long ones if possible so as not to put the vendor under unreasonable pressure. You may be able to split the task into distinct stages such as pulling the cables one weekend, installing the equipment on another and testing the network on the final weekend. Whether or not you need to do this depends upon the size and complexity of the project and the capability of the vendor. Don't overdo it, because the staging activity can increase the overall installation costs.

Obtain an on-site network test plan from the vendor. Although the vendor can install test software that emulates the maximum numbers of concurrent users on the network, there may be tests that require the involvement of one or more business staff. In order to satisfy contractual obligations the vendor will request that some of the key tests be witnessed by a nominated business staff. Be prepared to give up your weekends.

Technical Support

For commercial reasons the vendor will describe a separate support and maintenance arrangement. The level of technical support that you purchase will depend upon the level of computer expertise that you have in your business. Be aware though, that the level of technical support may be mandated by the certification body and you will have to meet the body's requirements in order to maintain computer system certification. The chapter *'Obtaining You Specified Needs'* contains example support and maintenance wording in the *Contract (Guide) Part 1.9 Equipment Maintenance.*

Obtaining Your Specified Needs

The Contract.

Define what you want though the contract. Most likely, it is the first document that the vendor will see from you, and its content will form a particular idea of your needs in the vendor's mind. It tells the vendor that your inquiry is genuine and warrants serious attention. The more care and effort you invest in the contract the closer the computer system will meet your expectations. For clarity, contracts for technological products are structured in four parts: the Introduction, consisting of a description of the parties involved in the commercial relationship, and how the contract came into being; the Contents and Definition of Terms; the Commercial Clauses, containing the legal obligations under which the contract will be conducted; and the Annexure, containing the Requirements Specification, the Project Plan, and Payment Schedule. Figure 8, The Contract Structure, shows a representation of this.

Is it Worth the Effort?

Writing a formal contract typically running into tens of pages is not a trivial task for a small to medium-size business. But the advantage of doing so is considerable. The process makes you think clearly about the business objectives you expect to achieve from a computer system, and the documented outcome of your thinking is available for future use. In addition the analysis of how you manage your business, gives you insight into where improvements may be made in the future. These improvements may not all be computer related, and can lead to general improvements dealing with customer satisfaction, administrative effectiveness and conformance to business regulations.

A Guide

I am providing a contract *guide* in this chapter since each jurisdiction has a legal framework that differs in subtle ways and affects the wording of the contract drawn up. Nevertheless, there are many common elements in an information technology contract that you should know about. This is so that you can effectively engage the services of a legal professional to help you compose the draft contract, and subsequently, negotiate that draft contract with the chosen vendor. You can create your information technology contract from a number of sources. Common sources are:

- Employ a legal professional who specialises in information technology contracts to raise a contract for you.

- Purchase a standard or model information technology contract from a consultant who specializes in this type of work. Use the consultant to tailor the contact to suit your needs.

- Approach your business association, or a government business help organisation, both who may have model information technology contracts devised especially for different business sectors. Note too, that these organisations sometimes have free or low cost legal advice available.

- Do it yourself if you have the expertise in-house.

Knowledge of the contents of a typical information technology contract, such as that contained here, will help you judge the quality of the above mentioned source material and create a contract to suit your needs and circumstances.

Obviously the size of the contract will depend upon the complexity of the system, the amount of financial risk you can take and the size of your business. The contract guide shown here is between forty and fifty pages long, the *commercial* section would be suitable for a range of business sizes, as it would not vary much with the technical complexity of the system. The size of the technical section would vary considerably between a small business occupying a single site and a larger company with branch offices widely distributed. An international business may need separate contracts for the jurisdiction of each country. Put simply, the size of the contract scales with the size of the computer system.

The section *'Purchase Order or Contract?'* in the chapter *'Management Issues and How to Get Started'*, helps you decide whether or not to raise a formal contract or use a purchase order for the procurement that you are about to make. The contract guide follows.

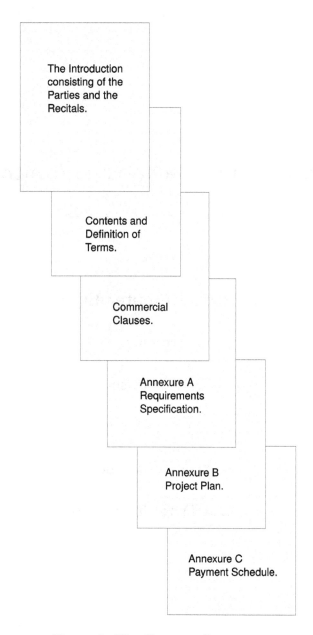

Figure 8: The Contract Structure

Information Technology Contract

Number [XXX-XXX-XXX]

For

Networked Computer Equipment

between

[Name of Business]

and

[Name of Vendor]

Issue Date: [dd.mm.yy]

Information Technology Contract (Guide)

Parties

This agreement is made between *[insert name of Business]* whose principal office is located at *[insert address and contact details of Business]* and *[insert successful Vendor's name]* whose registered office is located at *[insert successful Vendor's address and contact details]* and is licensed to conduct business in the design, installation, test and maintenance of general-purpose computer equipment and networks.

Recitals

The Business issued its requirements to potential vendors for the procurement of an information technology system conforming to the information contained in the Contract *[insert document number and issue date here]* and its Annexures A, B and C.

The Business evaluated the submitted responses from the vendors and selected the above named Vendor as the successful one. The Business has determined that entering into a Contract with the chosen Vendor will meet the Business's information technology needs as defined by the Contract and its Annexures A, B and C.

Therefore the Business awards the Vendor this Contract, the terms and conditions of which shall govern the behaviour of the Business together with the behaviour of the Vendor's design activities, operations and furnishings in relation to the Contract.

The Vendor shall supply the system described in the Contract at the times agreed in the Contract to enable the Business to use the system in the manner anticipated; in consideration of which the Business shall pay the agreed Contract price to the Vendor upon the completion of the works. Monies paid by the Business to the Vendor shall be in the manner described in Annexure C, Payment Schedule to the Vendor *[or other payment arrangements as agreed between the parties]*.

Guidance. *[If you want a harmonious relationship with your vendor, so staying out of court, then employ a legal professional to draw up your contract. There are two relationships to which you must pay constant attention: one, is the relationship between you and your legal professional, and two, is between your and your vendor. The quality of the latter depends somewhat on the quality of the former. Find a legal professional who will write a contract in plain English so that a non-legal professional can understand it. Help your legal professional by producing a description of the bargain (or deal) that you expect to take place. This can be in the form of a list or narrative outline derived from your Needs Analysis. Discuss 'what if' contract situations, so that you are prepared for the unexpected and minimise the commercial risks involved. You will also sleep more peacefully! Small companies, because of time constraints, may choose to accept the standard contracts of vendors. It's equally important here to do the preparatory work of Needs Analysis, so that you know which contract boxes of tick. Submit the vendor's small print to your legal professional.]*

Guide Contents

4.3 Vendor's Insurance

4.4 Severability

4.5 Waiver

Part 5 Disputes, Remedies and Limitation of Liability

5.1 Disputes and Remedies

5.2 Limitation of Liability

Part 6 Contract Termination

6.1 Termination for Contract Default

6.2 Termination by the Business

6.3 Termination by the Vendor

6.4 Termination Not to Affect Rights in Respect of Prior Contract Breaches

Part 7 Contract Administration

7.1 Section Headings, Incorporated Documents and Order of Precedence

7.2 Entire Agreement, Term and Survivorship

7.3 Independent Status of the Business and the Vendor

7.4 Governing Law

7.5 Subcontractors

7.6 Assignment

7.7 Publicity

7.8 Review of Vendor's Records

Part 8 Contract Execution

8.1 Authority to Bind

8.2 Signatures

Annexure A The Requirement Specification

Annexure B The Project Plan

Annexure C Payment Schedule to the Vendor

Definition of Terms

Acceptance Testing means the testing of the computer network over a period of time as an integrated system to demonstrate that it meets the characteristics described in the Standard of Performance, and where appropriate, the manufacturer's specifications for the installed software and equipment.

Confidential Information means information that is exempt or may be exempt from disclosure to the general public or other unauthorised persons under national, federal or state freedom of information laws. Examples of Confidential Information are social security numbers, email addresses, telephone numbers, financial and credit card information, drivers license numbers, medical records and data, law enforcement records, most computer code, and computer system security parameters *[modify the list as required by the Contract]*.

Contract means this document together with the associated documents listed in section titled *'Section Headings, Incorporated Documents and Order of Precedence'*.

Contracted Maintenance Service means a service agreement which starts after the computer network Warranty Period, and consists of an agreed level of maintenance activity by the Vendor to keep the Business's computer network operational to a predefined standard of operation. Typically the predefined standard of operation is that defined in the Requirements Specification.

Delivery Dates refers to the dates given in the Project Plan for the delivery of services and equipment procured through the Contract.

Equipment means the computer equipment specified in the Requirements Specification.

Failure to Perform means failure to meet the terms, conditions and obligations set out in the Contract.

Letter of Acceptance is a letter written by the Business accepting that, upon the evidence of the Vendor, that the installed computer network system has met the Standard of Performance set out in the Requirements Specification.

Business means the organisation, company or other legal entity that is procuring and has placed an order for the computer system from an information technology vendor.

Project Plan means a plan, list or diagram devised by the Business proposing a series of work activities and work objectives in relation to the passage of time and money for the implementation of the specified computer network system.

Representative means a person appointed by the Business and Vendor's organisations who will be responsible for the management of the Contact. The Representative is the primary contact person in each organisation in relation to the Contract activities. The title of the Business's representative is Project Manager *[or choose another title as appropriate to your Business]*.

Requirements Specification means a document raised by the Business describing the objectives, work needs, productivity outcomes, and network standard of performance which the computer network will be expected to provide.

Software means the source code or object code of the computer programmes given (in the case of open-source software) or licensed (in the case of proprietary software) to the Business from the Vendor in conformance with the Contract. Software includes the residence of object code in the equipment realised through different technological processes; it may be known as embedded code, firmware, internal microcode. New descriptions of object code resulting from technological development are included.

Standard of Performance means the criteria in the Requirements Specification that must be met over a specified period of time, before the computer network is deemed to have passed its Acceptance Tests. The criteria applies to all additional, replacement, modified or substitute Equipment unless otherwise agreed by the Business.

Subcontractor means a person, business or other organisation not in the employment of the Vendor who is engaged under a separate contract with the Vendor to carry out the whole or part of the Project Plan under the Contract.

System Administrator means a member of the Business who has the responsibility to operate the computer network after the system is fully implemented and operational.

Vendor means the successful bidder for the work described in the Contract, together with its employees, agents and subcontractors as permitted by the terms of the Contract.

Warranty means an undertaking by the Vendor to rectify free of charge any computer system non-conformance with the adopted design proposal put forward by the chosen Vendor in response to the business's request for a quotation.

Warranty Period means that period of time set forth in the Contract Section *'Equipment Warranties'* where the Vendor guarantees that the Equipment will be in good working order and conforms to the agreed specifications.

Part 1 Obligations of the Information Technology Supplier (Vendor)

1.1 Professional Standard of Care

The Vendor shall exercise reasonable skill, care and diligence in the performance of the Project Plan in accordance with the code of ethics and standards of conduct of the information technology profession. **Guidance**. *[Depending upon the industry sector in which you are operating, the vendor may belong to one of a number of business, trade or professional organisations. Each one of these has a code of ethics tailored to the industry sector which it represents. If you use your search engine to find 'My Code of Ethics' on the Internet; it has an extensive list of organisations together with their code of ethics for you to read.]*

1.2 Appoint a Representative

The Vendor shall appoint a person to act their Representative and make them known to the Business. The Vendor agrees that the person so appointed shall have the authority to act on behalf of the Vendor for all purposes in connection with this Contract.

1.3 Inform the Business of Matters Likely to Change the Scope or Timing of Services

If the Vendor becomes aware of any matter which will change or which has changed the scope or timing of the Service, then they will give timely notice to the Business and the notice will contain, as far as practicable in the circumstances, particulars of the change.

1.4 Knowledge of Business Requirements

The Vendor shall use all reasonable efforts to inform themselves of the Business's requirements for the Project, and shall consult with the Business for this purpose for the duration of the Contract.

1.5 Software Licence Grant

The Vendor warrants that it has the right to grant software licences to the Business through this Contract, either because the Vendor is the owner of the software, or it has the proprietary rights to commercially licence the software from the legitimate owner of the software. Where the software is open-source the Vendor shall uphold the conditions of the open-source licence. Licence in the software shall include at no additional cost, software interface modules to enable the different applications to work together, and software upgrades that provide enhanced functionality, performance improvements, increased security, error corrections or other changes that are logical extensions of the supplied software version.

The licence fees for future additional users of the software shall be the same as those charged through the Contract.

1.6 Confidentiality

The Vendor agrees to safeguard the Business's Confidential Information and not to disclose it to third parties without prior written permission from the Business.

1.7 Standard of Performance and Acceptance

After installation of the computer network the vendor shall demonstrate that it meets the performance characteristics stated in the Requirements Specification. The Vendor shall demonstrate the network's performance to specification during the concurrent use of all of the workstations on the network. The tests shall be so arranged that the test traffic loading on the network represents, as near as practicable, the realistic use of the network in the day-to-day operation of the business. Each workstation may be concurrently operated by the Vendor's test personnel or by appropriate emulation software supplied by the Vendor.

Since the *availability* (part of standard of performance) of the network cannot be demonstrated during the limited time taken by the performance testing, at this point the Vendor shall describe the means employed to meet the stated availability figure in the Requirements Specification. The means employed may include technological methods such as the use of fault-tolerant software, automated diagnostic self-test and reporting, and hardware redundancy though duplication; or the means employed may include the use of service methods such as continual help desk support, routine visits by the Vendor's service personnel, and short times-to-restore if the network breaks down.

The Acceptance Testing used to demonstrate the Standard of Performance shall be for a period of *[state the period of acceptance testing, this is typically ninety calendar days from the time the equipment is successfully installed and commissioned]*. If the system does not meet the Standard of Performance in the time stipulated, then the Business may at its discretion:

- Continue Acceptance Testing until the Standard of Performance is met or until the elapse of a further ninety calendar days, whichever is the sooner.

- If after one-hundred-and-eighty days the system has not met the Standard of Performance then the Business may, at its option, declare the Vendor to be in beach of this Contract and terminate it, or request a replacement system at no additional cost to the Business.

- At the successful completion of Acceptance Testing the Business shall send a Certificate of Acceptance to the Vendor and complete any outstanding payments as agreed and specified in the Payment Schedule shown in Annexure C.

1.8 Equipment Warranties

The Vendor warrants that each item of commercial-off-the-shelf equipment, firmware or software conforms to its published specifications, and that the integration of the items into a computer network meets the operational characteristics set out in the Requirements Specification. The Warranty shall be for a period of one year unless otherwise agree in writing.

1.9 Equipment Maintenance

At the end of the Warranty Period specified in the section Equipment Warranties above, the Vendor shall offer a Contracted Maintenance Service for the Equipment described in the Requirements Specification. The terms of the Contracted Maintenance Service shall be agreed between the Business and the Vendor and shall include the minimum service performance levels listed below. The maintenance charges agreed are set forth in *'Annexure C, The Payment Schedule'*.

- During the period of the Contracted Maintenance Service the Vendor shall keep the Equipment in good working order performing in accordance with the Requirements Specification, or with the Business's prior written approval performing to a lesser specification agreed between the parties.

- On-demand technical help-desk support to enable the Business's system administrator to manage the day-to-day operation of the computer network in good working order. Technical help-desk support shall be available for *[state the period of time that you require help-desk support to be available]*. The maximum Vendor response time to a help-desk request shall not be greater than *[one quarter-hour or other agreed time]*.

- Preventative maintenance for the purpose of keeping the network performing to its Requirement Specifications in the face of a changing network environment such as supplier software upgrades, new threats from malicious attacks and equipment degradation due to aging. The Vendor shall state the amount of time and frequency of site visits required to carry out these routine services, and the Business shall provide Vendor access for the performance of these services at a time convenient to both parties.

- Equipment repair when the network has malfunctioned or is inoperative, this service shall be available for *[twenty-four hours a day, seven days a week or other agreed times]*, and the response time from when the Business has informed the Vendor of the failure to the arrival of the Vendor's qualified field technician shall not be greater than *[two hours or other agreed time]*, the time to repair shall not be greater than *[eight hours or other agreed time]*.

The information of the network's failure shall be from a designated person within the Business such as a System Administrator.

At the conclusion of each maintenance visit the Vendor's field technician shall provide a maintenance activity report which shall include the following minimum information:

- The date of the service request.

- The date and time of arrival of the qualified field technician.

- The type and serial numbers of the equipment.

- The time spent working on the repair.

- A description of the malfunction or failure.

- A list of the parts replaced or additional software installed.

- Additional charges, if applicable.

1.10 Training

The Vendor shall provide training in the safe use and operation of the computer network equipment. The training shall be of sufficient depth to enable the Business's staff to operate the equipment in the required fashion with support only from the Vendor's help-desk facility, where provided. Training for specialised software applications outside of the Vendor's field of expertise shall be carried out by the help of appropriate sub-contractors by agreement between the Business and the Vendor.

1.11 Title to Equipment

In consideration of payment of Contract charges and software license fees, and upon successful completion of Acceptance Testing and the receipt of the Business's Letter of Acceptance and any outstanding monies, the Vendor shall convey the title of the equipment to the Business, free and clear of all liens, pledges, mortgages, encumbrances, or other financial security interests.

1.12 Shipping Risk and Loss

The Vendor shall safely transport the equipment specified in the Contract, freight prepaid, FOB at the Business's destination. The Vendor agrees to bear all risks of loss, damage or destruction of the equipment prior to the existence of the Business's Letter of Acceptance, except loss or damage attributable to the Business's fault or negligence.

1.13 Delivery

The Vendor shall deliver the equipment and software ordered in accordance with the Delivery Dates agreed on the Project Plan contained in Annexure B. For any exception to these delivery dates the Vendor shall notify the Business and obtain prior approval in writing. If the Vendor fails to meet the agreed Delivery Dates without agreement and approval then the Contract may be terminated or the Business may claim damages available under law.

Part 2 Obligations of the Business (Client or Purchaser)

2.1 Provide information, Documents and Other Particulars

When the Business awards the Contract, the Business shall make available to the Vendor all information, documents and other particulars relating to the Business's requirements for the Project.

2.2 Provide Access to the Business Premises

When the Contract Conditions are agreed between Business and Vendor the Business shall make arrangements to allow the Vendor to enter the Business and other lands as necessary to enable the Vendor to perform the Project Services.

2.3 Obtain all Necessary Approvals

The Business agrees to obtain all approvals, authorities, licenses and permits that are required from governmental, municipal or other responsible authorities for the lawful implementation and completion of the Project.

2.4 Appoint a Representative

The Business shall appoint a person to act as their representative (the Project Manager) and make them known to the Vendor. The Business agrees that the person so appointed shall have the authority to act on behalf of the Business for all purposes in connection with this Contract.

2.5 Inform the Vendor of Matters Likely to Change the Scope or Timing of Services

If the Business becomes aware of any matter that may change the scope or timing of the Project Plan, then the Business shall give written notice to the Vendor as soon as practicable under the circumstances.

2.6 Confidentiality

The Business agrees to safeguard the Vendor's Confidential Information and not to disclose it to third parties without prior written permission from the Vendor.

Part 3 Payment to the Vendor

3.1 Prices

The Vendor agrees to provide the products and services conforming to the Requirements Specification at the prices set out in *'Annexure C, Payment Schedule'*. No other moneys shall be payable to the Vendor.

3.2 Maintenance and Support Fees

When the Vendor-provided Equipment Warranty expires, and upon election by the Business to take up the Contracted Maintenance Service offered by the Vendor, the Business shall pay the maintenance and support fees to the Vendor at the prices set out in *'Annexure C, Payment Schedule'*.

3.3 Taxes

The Business will pay sales and service taxes, if any, imposed on the products and services acquired through the Contract. The Vendor shall pay all other applicable taxes.

3.4 Invoice and Payment

The Vendor shall submit itemised invoices to the Business's Project Manager. The invoices shall provide and itemise the following as applicable:

- The Business's Contract number.

- The Vendor's name, address, phone or other contact number, and the business's identification number required in the jurisdiction.

- Description of the products and services, including the quantity, model, serial numbers and version.

- Dates of delivery, installation and set-up.

- The price for each item, or the Vendor's list price for each item and any quantity discounts.

- Maintenance charges.

- Net invoice price for each item.

- Taxes.

- Shipping costs.

- Other charges.

- Total invoice price.

- Payment terms including any available prompt payment discounts.

If the Business fails to make a timely payment, the Vendor may invoice the Business *[state agreed percentage]* interest per month on the amount owing.

Part 4 General Provisions

4.1 Patent and Copyright Indemnification

The vendor shall warrant that the use of the Equipment and Software supplied under the terms of the Contract does not infringe any patent, design registration, copyright, trade secret, trademark or other proprietary right of a third party world-wide. The Vendor shall defend, indemnify, and save harmless the Business from and against any claims proceeding from the above mentioned infringements and bear the expense of defending any such claim.

4.2 Save Harmless

The Vendor while performing its Contractual duties, shall defend, indemnify and save harmless the Business from and against any claims by third parties arising from intentional, willful or negligent acts or omissions of the Vendor, its employees, agents or subcontractors.

4.3 Vendor's Insurance

Guidance. *[In some jurisdictions, industrial insurance law directs the purchaser to assume responsibility for ensuring that the Vendor has insurance cover that complies with industrial law. If the responsibility for insurance is not mandated by law, it would be prudent for the Business to determine the insurance categories and financial limits of cover needed by the Vendor to protect the Business from Contractual risks assumed by the Vendor. Since the type and scope of insurance needed for each Contract will vary between jurisdictions, the list below is a guide based on the typical needs of information technology contracts. Get professional help on insurance matters so that your understand the risk to your business.]*

The vendor shall, during the Contract term, and beyond where agreed, purchase and maintain the insurance described in the list below in this section. The type and scope of insurance shall be agreed between the Business and the Vendor and form part of the Contract. If the specified Vendor's insurance is invalidated in any way, the Vendor shall provide written notice of such invalidation to the Business within one business day of receiving the invalidation notice. Failure to purchase and maintain the specified Contact insurance, may at the Business's sole option, result in this Contact's termination.

- Commercial General Liability. **Guidance**. *[This policy covers four types of claim (made by the Vendor or its employees): bodily injury (including death) resulting in physical harm or loss of faculties, property damage or loss, personal injury (loss of reputation) such as slander or libel and advertising injury (false claims in advertising). The insurance should be worded so that it includes damages, legal defense fees and settlement charges to be borne by the insurer. The bodily injury cover applies to accidents in the Vendor's place of business and at your Business. The property damage cover will include fire, theft and other means of loss applying to furniture, computers, office equipment and materials also at the Vendor's place of business. The Vendor may need (at your request) to extend the basic cover to include data, papers, records and securities at the Vendor's place of business. You can describe this type of insurance in the Contract as shown here.]* Commercial General Liability with policy limits not less than a Combined Single Limit for Bodily Injury, Property Damage and Personal Injury Liability of *[state the amount here]* per occurrence and *[state the amount here]* aggregate.

- Workers' Compensation and Employer's Liability. **Guidance.** *[(This cover is sometimes specified by law or regulation, so check the statutory requirements for your jurisdiction.) Workers compensation covers the Vendor against employee claims for on-the-job injuries or work-related illness. Employer's liability protects the Vendor in the event of an employee alleging that the employer's negligence or failure to provide a safe workplace was the cause of the employee's injury or illness. You can describe this type of insurance in the Contract as shown here.]* Workers' Compensation and Employer's Liability as required by law or regulation. It shall be provided in amounts not less than *[state the amount here]* per incident for bodily injury by accident, *[state the amount here]* policy limit by disease, and *[state the amount here]* per employee for bodily injury by disease.

- Business Vehicle Liability. **Guidance.** *[This covers the risks of bodily injury (including death) and property damage caused by the commercial use of the Vendor's owned, hired or non-owned motor vehicles. You can describe this type of insurance in the Contract as shown here.]* Business Vehicle Liability cover for bodily injury, property damage and vehicle contractual liability applying to owned, hired, and non-owned vehicles. The combined single limit of liability for each vehicle accident shall be no less than *[state the amount here]*.

- Umbrella Policy or Excess Liability Policy. **Guidance.** *[Provides additional coverage if the limits of the primary commercial policies above are exceeded. It does not generally apply to the Worker's Compensation or the Professional Liability Errors and Omissions or the Commercial Crime insurance described below. You can describe this type of insurance in the Contract as shown here.]* Umbrella Policy or Excess Liability Policy for no less than the amount of *[state the amount here]*.

- Professional Liability Errors and Omissions. **Guidance.** *[This insurance protects the Vendor against claims for professional malpractice and failing to perform contractual obligations in a timely manner. Malpractice means professional negligence or failing to perform professional duties using best-known engineering practice and accepted standards of care. You can request this type of insurance to stay in force for some years after the Contract is completed, as some hardware and software design defects take time to show up on a computer network. You can describe this type of insurance in the Contract as shown here.]* Professional Liability Errors and Omissions covering the risks of professional malpractice and failure to meet the contract conditions with a coverage not less than *[state the amount]* for each occurrence and not less than *[state the amount]* general aggregate. The Vendor shall maintain this insurance for *[state number of years]* after the completion of the Contract.

- Commercial Crime. **Guidance.** *[This is to provide the Vendor with cover against employee criminality, such as stealing money, equipment or other assets from the Vendor or its clients (You). This cover should include computer fraud, and malicious or surreptitious code. You can describe this type of insurance in the Contract as shown here.]* Commercial Crime covering risks in the categories of computer fraud, malicious or surreptitious code, forgery, money and securities, and employee dishonesty. Commercial crime cover shall be *[state the amount here]*.

The Vendor shall pay the premiums on all the specified insurance policies. The insurance policies shall name the Business as an insured party on all general liability, automobile liability, and umbrella policies. Each policy shall bear this Contract number *[insert the contract number here]*.

Where the Vendor engages subcontractors, then the Vendor shall include the subcontractors in the specified insurance policies or shall provide copies of separate certificates of insurance taken out by the subcontractors. Each subcontractor shall comply with the contractual insurance requirements stated herein, and failure of the subcontractor to do so does not limit the liability or responsibility of the Vendor.

The Vendor shall provide to the Business all the certificates of insurance specified in this Contract within *[specify the number of days]* of this Contract's effective date. In addition the Vendor shall provide copies of renewal certificates of the specified insurance no more than *[specify the number of days]* after they become due for renewal. If the Vendor fails to provide evidence of insurance coverage as specified herein, then this may result in, at the Business's sole option, the termination of this Contact.

By specifying the insurance herein, the Business does not represent that coverage and limits agreed upon will be adequate to protect the Vendor's interests. The coverage and limits specified shall not limit the Vendor's liability under the indemnities and reimbursements granted to the Business in this Contract.

4.4 Severability

Any Contract term or condition held invalid shall not invalidate the other terms conditions and their application contained elsewhere in the Contract.

4.5 Waiver

The waiver of any breach of any term or condition shall not be deemed to be waiver of any prior or subsequent breach. Contract terms and conditions shall be waived, modified or deleted only in writing agreed and signed by the Contract parties.

Part 5 Disputes, Remedies and Limitation of Liability

5.1 Disputes and Remedies

If a dispute arises between the parties involved in this Contract and it cannot be resolved by direct negotiation between them, then it shall be handled by a Dispute Resolution Group in the manner following. Each party to this Contract shall appoint one member from their organisation to the Group. The appointed members shall jointly appoint an additional member from *[insert your jurisdiction's dispute resolution organisation here]*. The Dispute Resolution Group shall review the evidence such as the correspondence between the parties, the Contract terms, the applicable statutes and rules and resolve the dispute as quickly as practicable. The determination of the Dispute Resolution Group shall be final and binding on the Contract parties. The Business and Vendor agree to carry out their non-disputed contract responsibilities as if no dispute existed.

5.2 Limitation of Liability

The Business and the Vendor agree that they shall not make claims against one another for damages described in the list below, except for claims relating to bodily injury or death, fault or negligence, surreptitious code or intellectual property rights, such as an infringement of a patent, copyright or design, where these exceptions are set forth elsewhere in this Contract.

- Damages arising from causes beyond the their reasonable control such as, but not restricted to, acts of God, terrorism, war, explosion, fire, flood, earthquake, epidemic, quarantine restriction, strikes, freight embargoes, storms, and changes in government policy.

- Damages for delays without its fault or negligence unless the Contract equipment or service was obtainable on comparable terms from other sources in time to meet Contract schedule.

Part 6 Contract Termination

6.1 Termination for Contract Default

If either the Business or the Vendor fail to meet their significant Contractual obligations in a timely and proper manner, then the aggrieved party shall give the other party written notice of such failure. The party at default shall correct the failure within *[state the number of days here, typically thirty calendar days]*. If the failure is not corrected in the stated time, the Contract may be immediately terminated by the aggrieved party by written notice from the aggrieved party to the defaulting party. The aggrieved party shall have the sole discretion to terminate the Contract.

If the Business terminates the Contract because the Vendor is at fault, then the Business shall have the right to procure the products and services specified in the Contract on the open market. The Vendor shall be liable for all damages inflicted upon the Business by reason of the additional procurement costs including, but not limited to, those in the list below:

- The difference in cost between the original products and services described in the Contract and the replacement products and services.

- The administrative costs attributed to the costs of reviving the competitive bidding process such as the cost of mailing, advertising, reviewing, new document preparation, and negotiating a new contract with an alternative vendor.

- Any other direct costs resulting from the Vendor's default, such as retraining staff.

If the default of either party is beyond that party's control, fault, or negligence, this section shall not apply.

6.2 Termination by the Business

The Business may terminate the Contract if there is a change of management control of the Vendor, such as the appointment of a liquidator or receiver or take-over by another organisation, where it may be reasonably anticipated that it will have a detrimental effect on the Vendor's ability to perform its obligations under the Contract. The termination of the Contract shall be in writing by the Business to the Vendor, and the effective date shall be as stated in the termination document.

6.3 Termination by the Vendor

The Vendor may terminate the Contract if there is a change of management control of the Business, such as the appointment of a liquidator or receiver or take-over by another organisation, where it may be reasonably anticipated that it will have a detrimental effect on the Business's ability to perform its obligations under the Contract. The termination of the Contract shall be in writing by the Vendor to the Business, and the effective date shall be as stated in the termination document.

6.4 Termination Not to Affect Rights in Respect of Prior Contract Breaches

Contract termination shall be without prejudice to any prior claim that either party may have against the other in respect of any breach of their Contract obligations that occurred prior to the date of termination.

Part 7 Contract Administration

7.1 Section Headings, Incorporated Documents and Order of Precedence

The section headings in this Contract document are inserted as an aid to the understanding of the document by the reader, and shall not control or affect the meaning or construction of any of the sections.

Each of the four documents shown in the list below shall be treated as incorporated into this Contract and form part of the Contract obligations:

1. Annexures A, B and C dated the *[insert document dates here and keep them current]*.

2. The selected Vendor's response to the Request for a Quotation dated the *[insert document date here and keep it current]*.

3. All the Vendor's and supplier's publications, such as schedules, charts, diagrams, tables, technical documents, and any other supporting media used to demonstrate the Vendor's capacity and capability to carry out the Contract.

4. Written communications between the Business and the Vendor consisting of amendments, alterations, additions, modifications and waivers.

If there is any inconsistency between different sections in the Contract or between different documents making up the Contract or between the Contract and applicable Law, then the inconsistency shall be resolved in the following order of precedence:

1. Applicable national, federal or state statutes, laws and regulations.

2. Sections of this Contract.

3. Annexures A, B, and C.

4. The Request for a Quotation.

5. The chosen Vendor's response to the Request for a Quotation.

6. All the Vendor's and supplier's publications, such as schedules, charts, diagrams, tables technical documents, and any other supporting media used to demonstrate the Vendor's capacity and capability to carry out the Contract.

7.2 Entire Agreement, Term and Survivorship

This Contract and its legitimate written amendments, alterations, additions, modifications and waivers comprise the entire agreement between the Vendor and the Business and represents the obligations and commitments freely entered into by the parties and shall be binding upon them.

Legitimate alterations, additions, modifications and waivers on any part of the Contact shall be effective and binding only when in written form and agreed by the Representatives of both parties.

This Contract shall commence upon its signing by the involved parties and its term shall be governed by the activity and task completion dates agreed in the Project Plan shown in Annexure B.

The terms, conditions and warranties contained in this Contract which by their nature of practical application are intended to survive the completion, cancellation or other mode of Contract termination, shall so survive. The sections that shall survive the termination of the Contract are Confidentiality, Equipment and Performance Warranties, Software License Agreements, Patent and Copyright Indemnification, Disputes, Limitation of Liability and Publicity.

7.3 Independent Status of the Business and the Vendor

Each party involved in the performance of this Contract will be acting as an individual business or corporate entity and not as agents, employees, partners, joint venturers, or associates of one another.

7.4 Governing Law

The governing law that applies to this Contract is the law of *[name your jurisdiction here]*.

7.5 Subcontractors

The Vendor may enter into subcontract agreements with third parties for the performance of parts of the Contract, only with prior written permission of the Business. This permission shall not be unreasonably withheld by the Business.

The Vendor shall remain liable for any loss or damage to the Business under the terms of the Contract caused by the Vendor's Subcontractors, and the Vendor shall ensure that its Subcontractors honour the terms and conditions of the Contact.

7.6 Assignment

Both the Business and the Vendor may assign this Contract to another entity with the prior written permission of the other party. The assignment shall not relieve either party of its duties, obligations or default remedies available under the Contract.

7.7 Publicity

The Vendor shall not use the existence of the Contract to promote, publicise, or advertise its capacity or capability to conduct business without the prior written consent of the Business.

7.8 Review of Vendor's Records

The Vendor and its Subcontractors shall generate books, documentation and records to demonstrate compliance with the terms and conditions of the Contract. This information shall be safely retained for a period of *[state the statutory time period]* years.

The Business shall have access to the Vendor's and Subcontractor's information relating to compliance with the terms and conditions of the Contract. Such access shall be subject to reasonable times and the prior consent of the Vendor or its Subcontractors.

Part 8 Contract Execution

8.1 Authority to Bind

The signatories to this Contract declare that they have the authority to bind their respective organisations to this Contract.

8.2 Signatures

The parties whose signatures appear below, having read and understood this Contract and its attachments, do agree to its contents and execution and indicate their concurrence by setting their signatures below.

This Contract is effective this *[day]* of *[month]* of the *[year]*.

Approval by Business

Signature

Name and Date in Capitals

Approval by Vendor

Signature

Name and Date in Capitals

Witness 1 (Increase the number of witnesses as required by the jurisdiction)

Signature

Name and Date Followed by Address In Capitals

Information Technology Contract

Number [XXX-XXX-XXX]

For

Networked Computer Equipment

Annexure A

The Requirements Specification

Issue Date [dd.mm.yy]

Requirements Specification

Introduction

Our organisation is a business called *[name of your business]* staffed by *[number]* industry professionals, *[number]* production operatives and *[number]* clerical staff. We conduct our business in general purpose offices at the address given in the Contract section headed *'Parties'*. Our offices are located in a light industrial park in a neighbourhood that is is largely residential with a smattering of small retail businesses. There is a mature telecommunications network available in the area, including mobile phone and broadband network facilities. The district is well served by road and rail leading to major cities.

The managerial demands placed upon us to meet increasingly detailed business regulations, such as those of privacy, safety, financial, competition from other businesses, and the rising service expectations of customers; call for an integrated computer system to enable us to manage information in a way that satisfies this complex business milieu. The business information shall be in a central repository, structured in a way that mimics the organisational structure of the business, enabling uses in each specialization to access information which is appropriate to the task they are carrying out.

It is important that the computer system assists us in our business objectives, so that we can build a financially sound business while keeping the administrative burden minimised in relation to our business activities. Therefore ease-of-use is a key feature of the proposed system.

We expect the business to expand by an amount of *[insert amount of expansion]* during the next *[number of years]*. This will necessitate the addition of *[number]* additional business staff, so the system needs the ability to expand without operational disruption. We expect the system to remain operational for five years without major upgrades. The desired characteristics are shown in this specification.

Our staff are computer-literate and well educated, successfully passing though the national government school system, with technical and other specialized staff holding diploma and degree level qualifications. Therefore staff training can be flexible using different methods to take account of on-going business demands. Training methods can include traditional classroom presentations together with electronic methods, such as videos, films, and interactive computer training.

Network Description

Guidance. *[When you have progressed though the business processes described in* 'Management Issues and How to Get Started'*, then specify the computing equipment and software required at each workstation by examining each task to be carried out there. Typically each workstation will run a computer operating system supporting the software needed for that position and, in addition, the peripheral equipment needed to operate the workstation. State where there is more than one user operating each workstation (because you'll need a multi-user operating system). Produce a list to cover all the workstations as shown below. Include mobile workstations such as laptops, tablet PCs, and hand-held personal digital assistants.]*

Schematic Layout

Attached drawing number XXX-XXX-XXX shows the schematic layout of the proposed network.

Physical Layout

Attached drawing number XXX-XXX-XXX shows the building plan and the proposed positioning of the new workstations.

List of New Equipment and Applications

Networked computers and software comprising (for example) of:

Workstation N1: Reception (Two users)

Hardware

- One workstation computer supporting the network operating system and applications software.

- One visual display unit (monitor).

- One keyboard for data entry.

- One pointing device (mouse) for human interaction with the installed software.

- One local printer for producing documentation.

Software

- One network operating system.

- One sales order processing application.

- One office productivity suite.

- One Intranet and Internet email application.

- One office scheduling and planning application (for information on business meetings and absent staff).

- One Internet browser.

Workstation N2: Administration

Hardware

- One workstation computer supporting the network operating system and applications software.

- One visual display unit (monitor).

- One keyboard for data entry.

- One pointing device (mouse) for human interaction with the installed software.

- One printer for producing local documentation and acting as the networked shared printer (for the larger print jobs).

Software

- One network operating system.

- One financial and accounting application.

- One office productivity suite.

- One Intranet and Internet email application.

- One office scheduling and planning application.

- One Internet browser.

Workstation N3: Purchasing

Hardware

- One Workstation computer supporting the network operating system and applications software.

- One visual display unit (monitor).

- One keyboard for data entry.

- One pointing device (mouse) for human interaction with the installed software.

- One local printer for producing documentation.

Software

- One network operating system.

- One sales order processing application.

- One Intranet and Internet email application.

- One office scheduling and planning application.

- One Internet browser.

Workstation N4: Inventory Control

(and so on).

Servers

Guidance. *[Specify here how you want to manage your servers. There will be at least one server on the local network. The network services that the server is required to provide are described in this specification. State whether you wish to manage this server yourself or have the vendor manage it for you in a maintenance contract. If you want a business Internet site, then again, you have two choices; run the Internet site on an Internet server of your own, or purchase a managed Internet site on a private company's server (a hosted Internet service) for a monthly subscription. In both cases you will also need a separate Internet site content provider to design and maintain your business's presence on the Internet.]*

The number and type of servers shall be decided by the Vendor to provide the services specified in this requirements specification. At the end of the guarantee period the LAN server or servers shall be maintained by the Vendor.

The Company's Internet site shall be provided by others on a separate hosted Internet server.

Hardware

Workstation Visual Display Units

The visual display unit shall enable the computer operator to see the machine's alfa-numeric output response to data-input through the computer's data entry devices. Its specific characteristics shall, to facilitate comfortable viewing of the computer visual output, be as follows:

- The minimum size of the screen shall facilitate a full page display of documents of size *[state your document size here]* in portrait and landscape view.

- The display image shall have no perceptible jitter, swim or flicker. The luminosity of the screen shall be even. The screen resolution shall allow the viewer to recognise 8 point text at a viewing distance of 500 mm (black character on white background).

- The display image shall be readable without excessive glare, reflection, distortion or colour shift at viewing angles (up, down, left and right) of 70 degrees arc from the normal.(i.e. 30 degrees arc between viewer's line of sight and the screen surface)

- In addition to black and white, the display shall render its images in colour where the computer operating system and applications software generate colour output signals.

- It shall be possible to adjust the visual characteristics of the display image such as brightness, contrast, vertical position, horizontal position, aspect ratio, colour temperature, hue, saturation, and white balance (red, green, blue levels) so that the display unit may be used comfortably in a variety of business conditions. The adjustments may be though physical controls (buttons, sliders or on-screen displays [ODS]).

- There shall be mechanical arrangements to enable the screen to be adjusted in height by an amount of 150 mm, to be swiveled by an amount of plus and minus 45 degrees arc from the normal, and to be tilted down minus 5 degrees arc, and up plus fifteen degrees arc from the normal.

- The visual display unit shall be mechanically stable and positional adjustments shall be comfortably made by the viewer whilst seated in the viewing position.

- The mean time between failure shall not be less than 50,000 hours.

Keyboard

The keyboard shall enable alfa-numeric data to be entered into the computer operating system and its applications and to control the position of a text cursor where text is the mode of operation of the application in use.

Its specific characteristics to aid the task of data entry shall be as follows:

- It shall be a separate input device, but may consist of separate parts due to its ergonomic design.

- English shall be the language of the keyboard symbols and interpretation.

- Key layout shall be *[QWERTY]* with key placement corresponding to the *[US International standard]*.

- The top surface of the keyboard and its keys shall be non-reflective. The colour of the keyboard and its keys shall not be a distraction to the operator.

- The spatial positioning of the key groups and the orientation of the keys shall be ergonomic to facilitate comfortable operation of the keyboard during data entry.

- The front edge for the keyboard (facing the operator the 'ZXC... row') shall not be greater than 20 mm in height. The slope (rear edge raised) of the keyboard shall be adjustable within the range of 0 degrees arc to 15 degrees arc.

- When operating each key, a mechanical tactile feedback mechanism shall indicate the successful completion of the keystroke. The preference is a click.

- A left-handed version of the keyboard shall be available (numerical data entry keypad on the left-hand side).

- The size of the keyboard shall not exceed 500 mm (long) x 80 mm (wide) x 30 mm (thickest point away from the operator).

- Communication with the computer may be by cable, wireless or infrared. If batteries are required then they shall be of a standard readily available type, and able to be replaced by a non-technical person. The minimum battery life shall be *[three months]* with the keyboard operating *[forty hours]* a working week. There shall be an alarm indicator showing when the battery needs replacing before it expires and renders the keyboard inoperative.

- The keyboard shall withstand a workload of *[120 words per minute]*, maintained for *[4 hours]* a day for *[300]* days a year without requiring repair or replacement for a minimum period of *[two]* years.

Pointing Device (Mouse)

The mouse shall enable an independent moving cursor to be moved anywhere on the computer display screen to select the various functions and operations made available by the operating system and applications graphical user interface(GUI). It shall also be able to create line drawings and diagrams when used with the appropriate applications software.

Its specific characteristics are described below:

- The input buttons, keys or scroll wheels on the device shall be ergonomically positioned to enable the operator to use the device for long periods (hours) without experiencing physical discomfort.

- There shall be two input buttons and a central scroll wheel. The left-hand button shall select the GUI primary actions and the right-hand button shall select the GUI secondary actions. Rolling the central scroll wheel shall control the applications vertical scroll function and sideways pressure shall control the applications horizontal scroll function. The scroll wheel may have a third click function, depressing the scroll wheel may select GUI specialized actions where required by the applications software.

- The mouse movement and the resulting cursor movement ratio shall be adjustable through the mouse application software installed.

- A left-handed version shall be configurable though the mouse application software installed.

- The input buttons shall have a mechanical tactile feedback mechanism which indicates the successful completion of the operation. The preference is a click.

- If the mouse becomes contaminated and the contamination inhibits normal operation, then it must be able to be cleaned to restore it to normal operation.

- Communication with the computer may be by cable, wireless or infrared. If batteries are required then they shall be of a standard readily available type, and able to be replaced by a non-technical person. The minimum battery life shall be *[three months]* with the mouse operating *[forty]* hours a working week. There shall be an alarm indicator showing when the battery needs replacing before it expires and renders the mouse inoperative.

Workstation Printer

The workstation printer shall process printer requests from a client workstation. Its characteristics to meet the user's printing needs shall be as follows:

- Use the appropriate characteristics from Network Shared Printer shown below.

Network Shared Printer

The network shared printer shall concurrently (by queuing print requests and data) process the printer requests from all the network client workstations and servers. Its characteristics to meet the user's printing needs shall be as follows:

- The output shall be black, white and colour.

- Paper sizes: *[A4 (297 mm by 210 mm)]* and *[A3 (420 mm by 297 mm)]* as specified by the International Standards Organisation (ISO).

- Paper weight: *[64 g/m²]* (grams per square meter) to *[188 g/m²]*.

- Automatic double-sided printing (duplex).

- Print speed: *[30]* pages per minute minimum, text, at *[eighty per cent]* page coverage (that is, there shall be margins) at a black and white resolution of *[600]* dots per inch.

- First input paper tray *[A4]*, capacity: *[500]* sheets minimum.

- Second input paper tray *[A3]*, capacity: *[500]* sheets minimum.

- Output image type: text and business images (spreadsheets, diagrams, graphs and marketing colour images).

- Resolution: minimum is *[600x600]* dots per inch (dpi).

- Image quality: black text shall be dense black, with font edges sharp, other images with gray shading shall be smoothly graduated, with no vertical or horizontal banding. There shall be no banding in colour rendition.

- The average load: *[5000]* pages per month.

- Peak load: The paper feed mechanism shall not mis-feed, such as mis-picking, skewing, creasing or jamming in the course of printing *[500]* sheets in an uninterrupted duplex print run. There shall be no degradation in the printed image during this print run. In other words, the efficacy of the printer shall not diminish when loaded with a demanding print job.

- Maintenance: Replacement consumables shall be available in one working day.

- Management: The printers configuration and working condition shall be accessible over the network for the purpose of printer management.

Scanners and Data Entry

The scanner shall provide the facility to transform written text or composed images on paper copy to electronic representations (electronic files) which can be processed by the computers on the network. The associated software shall provide optical character recognition (OCR) to enable the text to be editable in its electronic form. The characteristics of the scanner to meet the user's scanning needs shall be as follows:

- Paper sizes: *[A4 (297 mm by 210 mm)]* as specified by the *[International Standards Organisation (ISO)]*.

- Paper weight: *[64 g/m² (grams per square meter)]* to *[120 g/m²]*.

- The duty cycle: *[1000]* pages per month.

- Manually loaded, duplex automatic document feed (ADF) of capacity *[50]* sheets of *[80 g/m²]* paper weight.

- Peak load: The paper feed mechanism shall not mis-feed, such as mis-picking, skewing, creasing or jamming in the course of scanning [50] sheets in an uninterrupted duplex scan run. There shall be no degradation in the scanner image during this scan run. In other words, the efficacy of the scanner shall not diminish when loaded with a demanding scan job.

- Output file image format shall include *[PDF, JPG, BMP, TIFF, compressed TIFF, TXT, ODF, HTML, RTF, FPX, PNG, PCX, GIF]*.

- The electronic file output of the scanner shall be accessible by all clients on the network.

- ADF minimum scan speed *[15]* pages per minute *[A4]* black and white text at a resolution of *[600]* dots per inch.

- Management: The scanner configuration and working condition shall be accessible over the network for the purpose of scanner management.

Servers

The server (or servers) shall consist of a combination of hardware and software that delivers the user software applications specified under the heading *'List of New Equipment and Applications'*.

It shall have the following general features to aid the operation and maintenance of the network:

- Convenient Hardware Maintenance. The main assembly of the server shall be built up of interrelated sub-assemblies. These shall be mounted in such a way that they are easily replaced in the event that they become faulty. The time taken to locate a sub-assembly fault, replace the sub-assembly, test and restore the server to normal service shall be no greater than *[four]* hours.

- Convenient Software Maintenance. The software running on the server shall be updated directly from removable storage media or downloaded from an appropriate Internet site.

- Straightforward Network Management. The server shall support LAN management software to enable the network administrator or vendor's technician to set up, configure and deploy network applications such as LAN messaging and collaboration services, shared external communication services and user application programs. The network management software shall also feature network intrusion detection, faultfinding and performance monitoring capabilities to aid the maintenance of the system.

- Fault Tolerance. The server shall by means of a suitable combination of software and hardware, provide fault tolerance features. These shall detect, capture and report errors occurring in the operation of the server, and ensure that none are allowed to go undetected to adversely affect the operation of the server. The server shall provide logically separated subsystems that prevent a failure in one from causing a failure in another. If one application crashes, the operating system and other applications shall remain intact, with a resulting increase in server reliability. Where possible, critical sub-systems, such as permanent memory, shall be self-healing, so that the defective sub-system may be replaced without interruption of service.

- Remote Access. The server LAN management software shall be able to deploy applications software to the portable devices of remote users. It shall be able to set up Internet access for remote users to provide, for example, email, office scheduling and planning and other applications running on the server (or servers). The remote access communication links shall be secure in operation. In addition, the systems administrator shall have remote access to the server for the purpose of setting up and deploying user services and monitoring network performance.

- Scalable. It shall be capable of expansion, enabling its network services to include [10] new users without the need for an additional server. Expansion shall be by means of the addition of hardware sub-assemblies and software modules, until the full capacity of the server is reached; at which point it shall be able to connect to one or more additional servers as required.

- Backup and Restore. The server shall provide data backup for itself and all users on the network (where applicable). The data backup media shall be removable so that a media set can be created, allowing individual data medium to be rotated to a specific backup method. For catastrophic system failure and data loss there shall be a complete backup image of the network user and system data, enabling the system administrator to restore the server and network to normal operation after the rectification of faults.

- Security. The server's resources shall be secure against unauthorised or malicious access. The system administrator shall have the ability to grant or deny user access to particular resources residing on the server. There shall also be protection against unauthorised or malicious intrusion from external networks to which the server is connected.

- Integrated management for the uninterruptible power supply (UPS). This feature shall manage operation of the *external* uninterruptible power supply. It enables the systems administrator to view the operational condition of the UPS such as: the completion (and results) of the UPS self-test routine; the charge state and remaining life expectancy of the battery; whether the input and output voltages are within tolerance limits and whether the internal temperature is within specification.

Software

General Characteristics

The software shall have its engineering design complete and be a commercially available and supported product. It shall be a current design with a remaining operational life of at least [7] years. Security patches and feature enhancement updates shall be available for the life of the product. The different types of software described in the sub-headings below shall form a single integrated software suite, where data in one application, where appropriate and required, shall be transferable to other applications.

Office Productivity Software

Guidance. *[Office productivity applications such as word-processors, spreadsheets, databases and drawing programmes are well-developed competitive products that compete in the market-place feature for feature. There is no significant difference between them as they are designed with a wide range of functions for general use. If you have dealt with computers as part of your professional training or business you may already have your favourite office productivity applications. Specify these as your preferred solution, since the major brands now run on a variety of network operating systems.]*

Network Operating System

The network operating system shall meet the general characteristics for software above and shall be suitable for operation on a multi-user local area network (LAN). It shall be capable of supporting concurrent use from all of the computer workstations and servers on the network. The software shall equip the server to provide user services and network management services specified in this document. It shall enable the users to interface with external wide area networks (WAN) such as those provided by commodity and product supply companies, and business financial or insurance organisations. There shall be capacity to allow for expansion in both the number of workstation users and the business customer base. The increase in the number of users is expected (for example) to be *[two]* over the next *[two]* years and the number of business customers is expected to increase by *[twenty per cent]* over the same period.

Network Security Software

A combination of security software combined with hardware shall provide protection against malicious intrusion of the network, its clients and servers. For privacy, data encryption shall be provided where appropriate and required. Security software shall consist of one or more applications providing protection against the following types of threat:

- Destructive computer viruses which incapacitate the network or exercise illegitimate secret control over a server or workstation, such as worms, trojans and root kits.

- Commercial intrusions such as advertiser spyware, diallers, sniffers and other malicious software, which may compromise the privacy of information on the network.

- Access though the workstations by users to unauthorised areas of information.

Note. Network security software shall not, in its operation, corrupt the legitimate user data residing on the network.

Guidance. *[Firewalls form part of network security. They may take the form of separate specialised hardware, be software as an integral part of a network modem-router, or be software as a part of a client's workstation. Network firewalls properly set up, block malicious network traffic; improperly set up, they can block legitimate traffic too. Be aware of firewalls. Occasionally some virus protection software, particularly 'on access' types which automatically virus-check files as they are opened can corrupt the opened file data. At the time of writing this seems to be a known problem with some email applications in particular. In addition, network security software can slow down the normal operation of network; ensure that the network performance testing is carried out with the network security applications in operation.]*

Specialist Software Applications

Guidance. *[Here we describe the applications needed by business specialists such as marketing, finance, accounting, stock control, supply chain, engineering, manufacturing, personnel, and others. You specify the software by completing the process described in the Chapter 'Writing the Requirements Specification', and under the headings 'An Example Derived from Business Needs' and 'Sales Order Processing (Example)'. The task is simplified where, as is common, specialists know from experience what software they need and what degree of integration is required with the overall system.]*

Network Performance

The network shall meet the performance parameters below, operating as a complete network with all its elements in concurrent operation. Each workstation shall be running one active application. (This requirement may be met with the use of specialized user simulation software).

Software Applications — Start-up Time

Software applications or single modules of modular applications shall appear and be operational at the workstations in less than *[five seconds]* after an application request.

Data Files — Transfer Time

A data file of *[5 MB]* shall be available at a workstation in a time not greater than *[1 sec]* after a workstation file request.

Specifying Data Backup and System Recovery

The backup system shall provide for the protection of business data during normal system operation, and complete system data recovery in the event of catastrophic system failure.

Normal Operation

In normal operation the system shall backup business data on the servers(s) and, where applicable, any distributed business data on the network. The data backup media shall be removable so that a media set can be created, allowing individual media to be rotated in a specific backup method. The backup system shall have the following characteristics:

- Network operation by backing-up files that are local or distributed across the computer network.

- Operation possible by a trained non-technical person.

- Provision of on-line help.

- Data compression to reduce the size of the backup files.

- User file selection for backup, restoration and file exclusion.

- Full, incremental or differential backup.

- Scheduling for unattended backup.

- User selectable data transfer error correction and reporting.

- Preservation of dated revisions saved by the user; selectable backup file overwrite, append to file or archive file.

- User selectable encryption for nominated backup files.

- Shredder tool for the elimination of selected unwanted files.

- Management of a wide range of backup equipment to allow for future changes in removable media.

Which Data

Specify here which data you want backed-up.

Guidance. [Produce an information tree (directory folder tree) which shows how you want the business data organized. Describe the data that you need backing up in terms of information needs, for example: email communications, business documentation, databases of business transactions. In a larger business, sub-divide the information into departments or divisions so that it is grouped by business activity type, then sub-divide again by subject. This will enable you to produce an information tree that will guide the vendor in constructing a file system directory tree on the server that suits your business . Show or refer to a picture of the information or directory tree.]

How Often

The frequency of the business data backup shall be: [Daily].

Backup Medium Capacity

Guidance. [If you want a simple daily manual backup procedure that uses only one backup medium during each backup process, or you want to automate the backup process without using an automatic media changer, then you need enough daily backup medium capacity to accommodate the day's full business data. Using the previous example under this heading in the section 'Defining Data Backup and System Recovery ':

daily business data generated at each workstation × number of workstations.
For example 200 MB × 6 = 1200 MB per day.]

The daily business backup medium capacity shall be: *[Specify here the daily business backup medium capacity]*.

Backup Time

The maximum daily business backup time shall be *[2 Hours]*.

System Recovery

For catastrophic system failure there shall be a complete rescue image of the network business and system data, enabling a system administrator to restore the server and network to normal operation after the rectification of faults. The restoration system shall have the following characteristics:

- The restoration process shall be by means of loading system rescue removable media (system rescue disk previously generated during system commissioning) and transferring a stored rescue image to the repaired network server(s).

- The rescue image may be stored on the LAN or at a distant reachable location on an external network.

- A current rescue image shall survive a catastrophic system failure.

During normal operation, the rescue image shall be updated at intervals of *[one month]* and after scheduled maintenance or upgrades of the operating system.

Total Permanent Memory Size (HDD)

Guidance. *[Using the previous example under this heading in the section 'Defining Data Backup and System Recovery ' the sizing the HDD capacity uses the expression below:*

$$daily\ data\ generated\ at\ each\ workstation \times number\ of\ workstations \times number\ of\ working\ days\ +$$
$$allowance\ for\ operating\ system\ +\ allowance\ for\ applications = total\ capacity.$$
$$For\ example\ 200\ MB/day \times 6\ workstations \times 220\ days\ +\ 7\ GB\ +\ 13\ GB\ =\ 284\ GB.]$$

The capacity of the permanent memory (HDD) shall be (with generous allowance for future expansion): *[500 GigaBytes]*.

Power Supplies

National (or state) utility mains supply at a nominal *[115/230VAC]* at a frequency of *[50/60 CPS]*.

The supplied computer equipment shall be protected against material damage from mains supply perturbations. Additionally, computer-data stored on the system shall be protected against loss or corruption from mains supply perturbations. Upon failure of the mains supply, data shall be automatically saved in a secure manner by the operation of a controlled network shut-down procedure. When mains supply restoration takes place, network operation shall be returned to normal by means of manual intervention.

Guidance. *[Typically manual intervention, but say if you want automatic re-start, or a combination of manual and automatic restart.]*

Reliability

Apart from scheduled maintenance, the network shall not be out of operation (downtime due to failure) for more than *[two occasions per year]* and for a duration of less than *[four hours]* on each occasion.

Guidance. *[Here we are principally talking about the server, because the computer peripherals, such as, printers, keyboards, pointing devices, drawing tablets can be quickly replaced without disrupting the entire network operation. Nevertheless, specify the whole network and let the vendor do the reliability arithmetic and offer a solution based on the vendor's experience and technical ability.]*

Connection To Outside Networks

The LAN shall have interfaces with the following WANs:

- The Internet.

- Business organisations, financial, scientific and engineering institutions.

- Business regulatory bodies.

Network User Access

The Network Operating System (NOS) management software shall provide a feature that enables the system administrator to select (allow or deny) user access to the resources furnished by the network. Table 6, User Access Rights, shows an example of the initial selection of user access rights (provide one table for each user).

Documentation

The vendor shall supply a Computer System Operating Manual, the minimum contents of which are listed below:

- Vendor information: contact and location details, document authorisation (sign-off) and arrangements for future version control (if any).

- A vendor statement that the supplied network system conforms to the product liability and health and safety legislation for the jurisdiction in which you operate. This statement shall appear in the manual front matter.

Individual User Permissions or Group Permissions: Y=Yes, N=No; Usr1=Create, Delete, Read/Write; Usr2=Read Only.

User Permissions and Network Resource Allocated	Reception	Administration	Sales	Purchasing	Stores	Engineering
User name issued	Y	Y	Y	Y	Y	Y
User password issued	Y	Y	Y	Y	Y	Y
Local printer	Y	Y	Y	Y	Y	Y
Shared printer	Y	Y	Y	Y	Y	Y
Customer records	Y, User2	N	Y, User1	Y, User2	N	N
Office Administration Files	Y, User2	Y, User1	N	N	N	N
Financial Files	N	Y,User1	N	N	N	N
Network configuration(System Administrator only)	N	N				
Internet	N, User2	Y, User2	Y, User2	Y, User2	Y, User2	Y, User2
WAN 1	Y, User2	Y, User2	Y, User2	Y, User2	Y, User2	Y, User2
And so on…						

Table 6: User Access Rights

- User CAUTIONS or WARNINGS which apply to the system. These shall appear in the manual front matter.

- A general description of the 'as installed' network; its topology, its equipment and installed software (including software version numbers). The network cables connection numbering system.

- A description on how to operate the network. How to safely start and log-on; log-off and shut down the network; with examples of normal network behaviour by means of screen shots, diagrams and symbols. An explanation of user access rights. How to use the data backup features and how to recover the network after a system crash.

- A technical description in simple language, but of sufficient depth to enable a (vendor independent) systems administrator to reconfigure the network after making changes or extending the network to accommodate new user requirements.

- The detailed configuration settings of each workstation, server and associated computing equipment. Each configuration shall include (where applicable): the administrative name of the product and serial number; the physical network address; the logical network address; and the type of network interface card. Other information as required to maintain the equipment such as internal switch positions and links.

- A description of the steps that the user can take to maintain the network in good working order.

- A list of supplier's associated user manuals required to operate the network applications software and network hardware.

- An explanation of the initial user access rights and user licensing arrangements for the installed software.

- A description of the warranties offered by the vendor and its suppliers.

Environmental Conditions

Guidance. *[The common office computer system is designed to operate in a benign office environment that is comfortable for office workers. During transportation it's protected by its packing and usually transported by specialist carriers who deal in sensitive electronic equipment. So the short specification below is sufficient. In the case of portables that are subject to rough treatment outside the office, you will need a properly designed carrying case. This is not as simple as you think, because many trendy or fashionable carrying cases provide little or no protection to their contents. If an effective carrying case is too cumbersome, you will need ruggedised equipment tested by the manufacturer to demonstrate that the equipment can endure spray, vibration and shock. The simplest approach is to specify the environment in which the portable is expected to operate and let the Vendor do the searching.]*

Ambient Temperature: operating *[5°C to 35°C]*; storage *[–20°C to 50°C]*.

Humidity: operating *[20% to 80%]* (non-condensing); storage *[5% to 90%]* (non-condensing).

Customer Privacy and Data Security

The computer system, its interface with external networks and its software shall comply with the regulations listed below in the jurisdiction of *[name the appropriate country or state]*.

- Customer privacy and data security regulations *[Replace with the proper names used in your jurisdiction, here and below]*.

- Health and safety at work regulations.

- Electro-magnetic compatibility regulations (prevention of electrical interference).

- National (or state) information technology improvement programmes that attract government funding for general business computerisation.

Computer System Certification

Alternatively the computer system shall comply with the business requirements for computer system certification of *[Name the certification body]* which encompass the above regulations and codes of practice.

Installation and Test

The vendor shall present a written test plan to the customer at the scheduled time on the project plan. The vendor shall factory test components of the system, assemble them, install them and implement the test plan on the completed network at the customer's premises. The completed system shall meet the requirements of this specification.

Technical Support

The vendor shall provide a description of the warranties provided by themselves and their suppliers. The warranties and the long-term maintenance arrangements are described in the Contract section *'1.8 Equipment Warranties and section 1.9 Equipment Maintenance'*.

Information Technology Contract

Number [XXX-XXX-XXX]

For

Networked Computer Equipment

Annexure B

The Project Plan

Issue Date [dd.mm.yy]

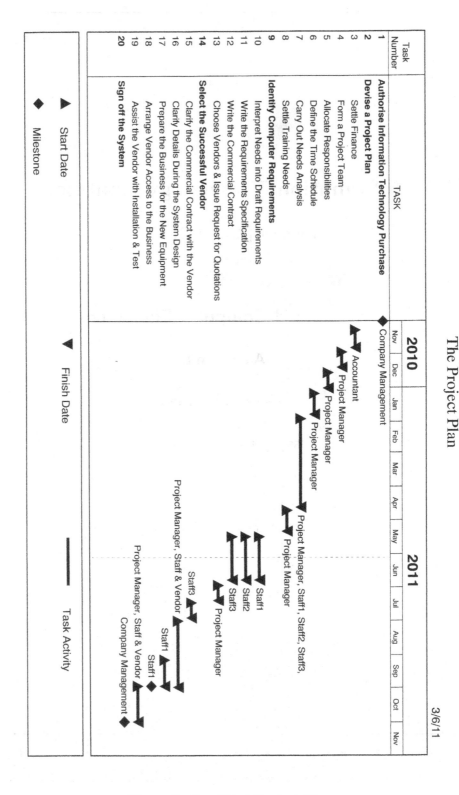

Figure 9: Simplified Project Plan

Information Technology Contract

Number [XXX-XXX-XXX]

For

Networked Computer Equipment

Annexure C

The Payment Schedule

Issue Date [dd.mm.yy]

The Payment Schedule

You arrange payment to the Vendor by negotiating a purchase or deal. The ideal from your point of view is to withhold the entire purchase price until the computer network system is commissioned, tested and formally handed over. This way the Vendor remains focused on the successful completion of your project, and is discouraged from diverting their attention away towards a more lucrative new contract elsewhere. If you are unable to strike such a deal, then propose that the agreed contract funds are placed into Escrow, and released to the Vendor at the completion of the project. Failing this you can propose that proportions of the total project fund be paid at agreed milestones on the project plan: but be warned that this arrangement is notoriously difficult to administer. It can take up a great deal of time discussing exactly what constitutes completion of a particular project task. Talk to your colleagues or your professional associations and obtain independent financial advice to solve the payment problem.

Managing Normal Operation

Policy and Procedures

The newly commissioned system is now ready for use. Having coped with the disturbance of installation and test by the Vendor, and accepted your technological acquisition as a working system, you now begin a somewhat unfamiliar work routine as you interact with the new software applications. At this point, to smooth the transition to the new work routine, and comply with your chosen information technology regulations (if any) you should have the following situation regarding computer system management policy and available user information for the operation of the system:

- One person (and, if possible, a stand-in) authorised to secure and administer the system and respond to system security breaches (or pay your vendor to do it).

- Arranged training for users in the security and operation of their applications.

- Written business policies on the authorisation, access, naming, storing, safety and disposition of office files both hard copy and electronic.

- Written user procedures on the creation of new files. These will contain information on how each new office file is identified (number and name), authorised, and where each file is located after creation. User file access is explained.

- Ensure there are Vendor-created user instructions for the security and basic operation of the system. For instance, what do users do in the event of their software freezing up, or the workstation becoming faulty in some other way: there should be an explanation of the basic actions that a user can take before approaching the system administrator.

With the policy and procedures distributed to users, there are routine tasks to be carried out by the system administrator. The routine tasks are:

- Arrange for the system to be attacked by a simulated malicious intrusion at a frequency recommended by the vendor for your business. Report results to interested parties.

- Use system security management tools to monitor the system for malicious intrusion at recommended intervals for your business.

- Update the virus protection, firewall software rules and application software patches as required to prevent malicious attacks against the computer system.

- Backup system files daily (or some other frequency as dictated by risk assessment and management policy). Keep a daily log of the backup process. Separately archive computer system audit files as specified by regulatory authorities (if applicable, that is you have elected to have a certified management system). There is more detail on backing up in the next section. Test the backup system at regular intervals: weekly, monthly, or as otherwise dictated by business policy.

- Shred discarded data (destructively erase) when a computer holding customer information reaches the end of its life. The normal file erase feature of servers and workstations does not immediately erase the data, it only makes it inaccessible to the system so that the erased file space can be overwritten later by new data. This makes the erased data recoverable to someone with expert knowledge and the appropriate software. You need data shredding software to permanently erase customer or other sensitive data on a computer destined for disposal.

- Allocate new user access rights or changing existing rights when needed.

- Automate log-off after a defined period of user inactivity.

- Encrypt data files and log files that are transmitted outside the business.

- Update the user applications when *worthwhile* improvements appear; otherwise resist pointless change.

- Carry out routine maintenance such as scan-disk, disk cleanup, and defragmentation, where required by the operating system.

- Keep software licenses current.

- Arrange for the computer system to be performance tested at regular intervals as recommended by the maintenance vendor and agreed in the maintenance contract. The vendor uses diagnostic software to carry out system performance testing.

- Contact the maintenance vendor for service when the system becomes faulty. Monitor the vendor's service performance. Keep the users informed about the operational status of the system.

As users become familiar with the operation of the system they will suggest improvements in the way they interact with the system and with one another. Arrange monthly meetings to consider user suggestions and agree on new ways of working together. This will ensure you develop the greatest benefit from your investment.

A Backup Method

The prevention of business data loss on your computer system depends upon the *repetition* of your chosen backup method. It is important that the method is simple, so that it does not become tiresome and lead to *abandonment*. Simplicity requires that a single removable medium have sufficient capacity to save all the network data during one backup session; this reduces the task of loading and unloading the media. To allow for the possibility of failure of the backup process itself, all effective backup methods use sets of backup media. The total number of backup media used also depends upon the *retention time*, which is the time that you want to keep the data in storage. Within a set, you rotate each piece of media in a particular sequence to give you the security and retention time that you need. Cost is also a factor.

Comprehensive backup applications intended for business use include features for both backing up business data and system recovery. So that when your network system is operating normally, you can restore business data when required; say, for instance, to replace corrupted or lost files or for the purpose of archiving selected data. The method below shows one way of doing this. If your system crashes, that is, it is no longer operating normally, you can restore it using the provided system recovery (bare-metal) features. The system recovery method is different from the business data backup method and depends upon the features of backup application software.

One common method suitable for a typical business data backup is the Daughter-Mother-Grandmother four-weekly media rotation (Widely known as the Son, Father and Grandfather method, but not in this book). This method is a realistic balance between security, convenience and cost. Assuming a five-day week and a retention time of one year, Table 7, Backup Removable Media Required, shows the number of medium sets required (you will need twenty items of removable medium).

Label the four daily-media as Daughter Daily 1 to 4; the three weekly-media as Mother Weekly 1 to 3; and the thirteen annual-media as Grandmother Four-Weekly 1 to 13. Carry out the method as follows:

Retention Time One Year		
Daughter	Daily	Four Removable Media
Mother	Weekly	Three Removable Media
Grandmother	Four-Weekly	Thirteen Removable Media

Table 7: Backup Removable Media Required

1. Do a full backup (all selected files) on Grandmother Four-Weekly 1 medium to get started. You will use this tape again at the end of the first cycle.

2. Use the Daughter Daily 1 to 4 media for the daily backup (incremental or differential) Monday to Thursday inclusive. Reuse these on the following weeks in the same way, overwriting the previous weeks data. The Daughter Daily media contain the youngest (most recent) data in the collection.

3. Use the Mother Weekly media 1 to 3 doing a full backup (all selected files) for three consecutive weeks in the four-week cycle. In this example you backup to the Mother Weekly media on three consecutive Fridays. On each consecutive four-week cycle you reuse the Mother Weekly media by overwriting. The data age is up to three weeks old — middle aged.

4. On the fourth week in the four-week cycle, do a full backup (all selected files) to the Grandmother Four-Weekly 1 medium again (only on cycle one). Do this with the remaining Grandmother media on every fourth Friday of each of the thirteen four-week cycles. Use new media each time until all thirteen media are used at the end of the year. Grandmother Four-Weekly media are not reused for thirteen months so the oldest data is thirteen months old.

Table 8, A Backup Method, shows how.

Keep a daily log of the backup activity so that you know exactly where you are regarding the media rotation. Use a business diary containing week numbers for the full year, and record each backup activity as you progress. Arrange the Grandmother Four-Weekly media numbering to correspond with the diary week numbers. This enables your stand-in to take over without confusion.

If you work more than five days a week, increase the number of Daughter Daily media to correspond to the total number of days that you work minus one. For a seven-day working week you will need six Daughter Daily tapes ending the working week on a Sunday doing a Mother Weekly backup. So long as you remember to change the removable media correctly between backup sessions, you can schedule the backup process to take place unattended: you don't have to be in the office. In addition, with the appropriate software, you can monitor the backup process over the Internet if you are at all apprehensive about the outcome.

To allow for natural disasters keep the completed Grandmother Four-Weekly media off-site in safe storage (fireproof, cool, dry and away from magnetic fields and

To get started do a full data backup on Grandmother Four-Weekly 1 medium.		
Week	**Day**	**Removable Media**
Week 1	Monday	Daughter Daily 1 (incremental or differential)
	Tuesday	Daughter Daily 2
	Wednesday	Daughter Daily 3
	Thursday	Daughter Daily 4
	Friday	Mother Weekly 1 (full backup — all selected files)
Week 2	Monday	Daughter Daily 1 — overwrite
	Tuesday	Daughter Daily 2 — overwrite
	Wednesday	Daughter Daily 3 — overwrite
	Thursday	Daughter Daily 4 — overwrite
	Friday	Mother Weekly 2 (full backup — all selected files)
Week 3	Monday	Daughter Daily 1 — overwrite
	Tuesday	Daughter Daily 2 — overwrite
	Wednesday	Daughter Daily 3 — overwrite
	Thursday	Daughter Daily 4 — overwrite
	Friday	Mother Weekly 3 (full backup — all selected files)
Week 4	Monday	Daughter Daily 1 — overwrite
	Tuesday	Daughter Daily 2 — overwrite
	Wednesday	Daughter Daily 3 — overwrite
	Thursday	Daughter Daily 4 — overwrite
	Friday	Grandmother Four-Weekly 1 (full backup — all selected files)
Repeat the cycle for thirteen weeks total: reuse the Daughter Daily and Mother Weekly media by overwriting; use new Grandmother Four-Weekly medium for each cycle, except for cycle one, where you will overwrite the initial backup on the Grandmother Four-Weekly 1 medium. Log your activity.		

Table 8: A Backup Method

electromagnetic radiation). In addition, rotate one Mother Weekly media off-site as you cycle though their backup sequence. Since data storage media is subject various kinds deterioration, establish the life of the media from the manufacturers and observe their recommendations.

The above method is one of many devised to suit different computing needs. Generally, as one would expect, the simpler methods afford less data security and the more complex greater security. In a typical business, the method you adopt may be mandated by an outside authority, such as a certification body or other national standards organisation; in this case you describe the method in the requirements specification to ensure you obtain a system that meets the appropriate regulations. The above method describes a backup schedule giving one years retention of data; statutory authorities regulate that specified data is to be stored for many years. To conform to the regulations, you carry out *supplementary backup*, taking off the specified data and archiving it on media separate from the annual medium rotation system.

Restoring Data

Using this method you restore business data as follows: when the Daughter Daily media is incremental, restore from a medium set consisting of the latest full data backup followed by all the incremental media since the last full data backup; when the Daughter Daily medium is differential restore from a medium set consisting of the latest full data backup and the last differential medium.

If You Cannot Bear It!

When many people first meet formal backup methods of computer data they enter a state of stupefaction; see their eyes glaze over! It all seems so overwhelming. Well, if you are a *small* business, say one or two people, generating small amounts of business data, megabytes rather than gigabytes each day, then you can adopt a simpler method than the one described above. This avoids the large number of removable media required by the Daughter-Mother-Grandmother method. Have one backup media for each working day of the week. Select the files that you want to back-up at the end of each day and carry out the backup process. In addition, transmit the day's business backup data to an Internet storage provider for off-site backup. Keep the separate system recovery image updated manually. For long-term storage use manual supplementary backup.

Entering Electronic Customer Records

How many paper customer records do you have stored in your business — one thousand; ten thousand; one hundred thousand? How well are the contents in each file organised? Transferring the hard copy customer data into electronic form is not a problem with an easy solution; this is a labour intensive activity and your regular staff are unlikely ever to have the time to complete it. The most direct method is to employ a data entry (keyboard) operator with experience in this field. Even so, an experienced operator will be employed with this task for some time. You can only enter alpa-numerics this way, not images, drawings, graphs or measuring instrument outputs. It may be possible to transfer the records by scanning some or all of the contents. If the alpa-numerics in customer records need to be editable in electronic form, then the scanning would have to be done by a specialist in the field, because popular scanning software applications transfer and store the data into non-editable images. If you planned for electronic customer records and decided to purchase a scanner workstation for regular use, you will be set up for entering initial records of new customers, but you still have the backlog of current customer records to enter, so again, you will need help. Disappointingly, this paragraph can only alert you to the necessity of allowing financial resources for this decidedly non-automated element of computer network implementation.

As Time Passes

As time passes society's expectations of the role of business people change. They react by devising fresh approaches and acquiring additional skills to satisfy customer demands. Statutory authorities regulate higher degrees of professionalism, demanding increased levels of record keeping and security. Computer technology develops to assist business people in meeting the demands placed upon them in the workplace. In several years time you will be thinking about updating your computer system, having acquired a deeper insight of the way it can help you. It's time again to consult this book.

Appendix A

Guide to General Terms and Conditions of Purchase

In the following terms and conditions the party to whom this purchase order is addressed is known as the Vendor and the party placing the purchase order is known as the Business.

Acceptance of Order. This purchase order is a request from the Business to be considered by the Vendor. The Vendor may signify acceptance by returning a written offer to the Business. If the Vendor is unable or unwilling to accept the request as set out in purchase order, and wishes to be considered for future orders, then the Vendor shall, in a timely manner, contact the Business, notifying it of the Vendor's inability or refusal to meet the request; or offer an alternative product or service. If the alternative product or service is suitable to the Business it shall issue a revised request, which, if accepted by the Vendor, shall be supplied. The Vendor shall not proceed with supply without confirming acceptance of the request with the Business. If the Vendor proceeds without confirmation of acceptance, the Business shall not be bound to take delivery of products or services or reimburse the Vendor for any cost incurred.

Price. The price stated on the front of this purchase order is firm and subject to variation only by written agreement between the Business and the Vendor or to a formula previously agreed in writing between the parties.

Packing. All products supplied under this purchase order shall be packed so as to ensure safe delivery into the Business's nominated delivery address. The packing costs shall be born by the Vendor.

Purchaser Supplied Materials. Unless specifically stated on the purchase order, all purchaser supplied materials or equipment for incorporation into the ordered product are included in the price and shall remain the property of the Business at all times, and shall not used for purposes other than the supply of the Business's order.

Delivery and Transportation. Products purchased under this order shall be delivered by the Vendor to the delivery address nominated on this purchase order.

Where the products are fragile, the Business retains the right to nominate shipping arrangements including the nomination of a carrier. The cost of delivery and transportation shall be subject to prior agreement between the Business and the Vendor and shall be specified on the face of the purchase order.

Standard of Acceptance. The Business shall be entitled to return any products to the Vendor if they do not comply with the specifications stated on or with the purchase order, or are not of merchantable quality. Products so returned shall be repaired, replaced or credited at the Business's discretion. The delivery and transportation costs of replacements for rejected products shall be shared equally between the Vendor and the Business unless otherwise agreed.

Terms of Payment. Unless otherwise agreed on the purchase order, payment shall be made by the Business to the Vendor thirty days after the end of the month during which delivery is accepted. The Vendor shall issue its invoice within seven days of delivery to the Business. All invoices must contain the Business's purchase order number.

Termination or Reduction of Order. The Business retains the right to cancel all or part of the procurement if the Vendor fails to deliver the products in accordance with the delivery schedule set out in the purchase order.

Assignment. The Vendor shall not assign this order to a third party without the prior written permission of the Business.

Whole of Agreement. This purchase order represents the entire agreement between the Business and the Vendor and no other terms or conditions shall have any effect unless in writing and signed by the Business's authorised representative.

Appendix B

Well you ought to know what to expect from a computer system administrator, whether you hire one from a vendor as part of a service contract, or hire one part-time or full-time on your staff.

Job Description—Computer System Administrator

Qualifications. Bachelor's degree in Computer Science or a related subject, or equivalent education and work experience. Operating System Certified Engineer an advantage. Significant knowledge of, or background in, integrated on-line systems, LANs/WANs, telecommunications networks and applications software. A minimum of one year experience with our operating systems, office applications, network management software, trouble shooting, configuration and security tools an advantage.

Responsibilities. Responsible for providing computer system services to the organisation's managers, supervisors, staff and customers. Manage the performance and maintain the security of the organisation's Local Area Network (LAN) and connected Wide Area Networks (WAN). Devise, implement and maintain LAN operating policies. Train staff in the correct use of the system. Keep abreast of emerging technology and advise the organisation on the current and future use of suitable hardware and software. Generate the Information Technology (IT) financial budget for current operations and future expansion.

Skills and Characteristics. To perform the job successfully, the System Administrator shall possess the following skills and characteristics.

Problem Solving. Identify and resolve problems in an organised and timely manner by gathering and analyzing information, and applying the scientific method. Develop alternative and novel solutions to recurring problems.

Oral Communication. Communicate clearly and persuasively while speaking to colleagues and associates; listen and get clarification; respond well to questions; participate in meetings by expressing points of view and presenting new ideas.

Written Communication. Write clearly and informatively; self-edit work for spelling and grammar; vary writing style to meet the reader's needs; present numerical data in a straightforward manner; read and correctly interpret technical documents and engineering drawings.

Change Management. Keep records of all server hardware and software upgrades and maintenance changes in the form of a change log. Implement system changes with the least disruption to the operation of the system. Tell the system clients what is going on regarding system changes and how it will effect them.

Quality Management. Support the organisation's quality programmes by generating quality plans relating to system performance (productivity, accuracy and usability).

Organisational Support. Follow the organisation's policies and procedures; complete administrative tasks correctly and on time; support the organisation's goals and values.

Strategic Thinking. In conjunction with the organisation's management team, develop IT strategies to support organisational goals; adapt the strategy to changing organisational conditions.

Judgment. Display willingness to make timely decisions; exhibit sound and accurate judgment under the prevailing circumstances; support and explain reasoning for the decision chosen; include the appropriate people in the decision-making process.

Planning and Organising. Prioritise and plan work activities; use time effectively.

Professionalism. Approach others in a tactful manner; react positively under pressure; treat others with respect and consideration regardless of their status or position; accept responsibility for one's actions; follow through on commitments.

Safety and Security. Observe safety and security procedures and ensure others are not put at unnecessary risk; use equipment and material in accordance with the manufacturer's instructions; understand and conform to the safety authority's regulations in managing the computer network.

Adaptability. Adapt to change in the work environment; manage competing demands; change your approach or method to best fit the current situation; deal positively with frequent change, delays, or unexpected events; be prepared to work outside normal office hours.

Dependability. Attend the workplace in a punctual manner. Work consistently under management direction; keep mentally and physically fit for work.

Conditions of Employment (Add the conditions of employment here)

Index

About the Author

Clive Libotte worked as an engineer in the avionics and process control industries. In England he was an electronics engineer with Elliott Flight Automation, a control systems analyst with Hawker Siddley Dynamics and a project engineer with Servomex Controls. In Australia he worked as an instrument and control engineer in the petro-chemical industry on construction projects with Woodside Offshore Petroleum, Flour Maunsell and Matthew Hall. He is an Incorporated Engineer(UK Engineering Council), and a member of the Institution of Measurement and Control.

www.ingramcontent.com/pod-product-compliance
Lightning Source LLC
Chambersburg PA
CBHW060145060326
40690CB00018B/3988